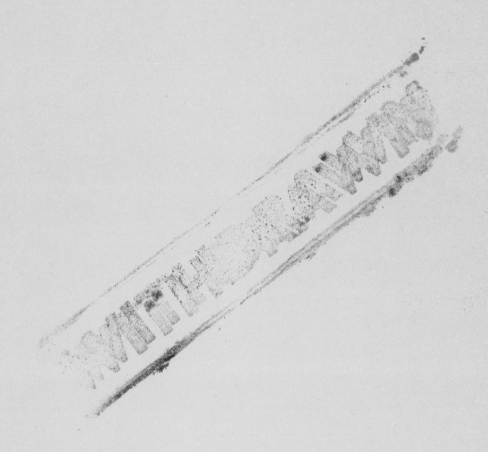

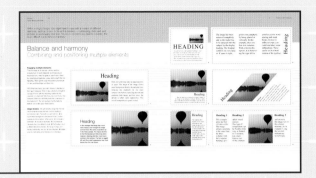

Design and Layout
Understanding and Using Graphics

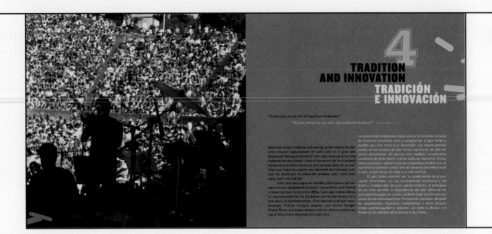

4
TRADITION AND INNOVATION
TRADICIÓN E INNOVACIÓN

"Latin jazz is an art of musical inclusion."

"El jazz latino es un arte de inclusión musical".

Design is a way of **looking** at and improving the **world** around us.

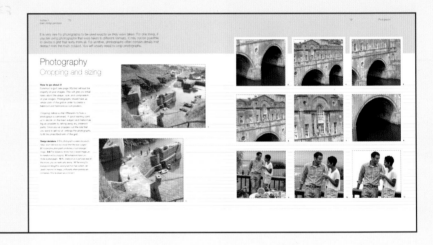

Photography
Cropping and sizing

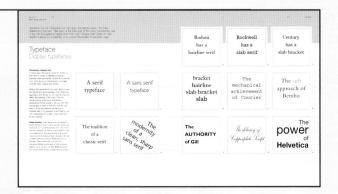

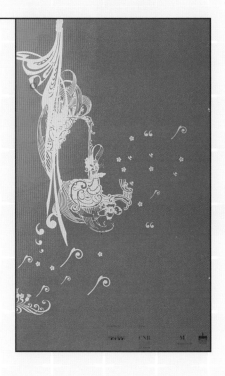

Design and Layout
Understanding and Using Graphics

David Dabner

BT Batsford

A QUARTO BOOK

Published in the UK in 2003
by B T Batsford Ltd
64 Brewery Road
London N7 9NT
www.batsford.com

A member of **Chrysalis** Books plc

ISBN 0 7134 8838 7

British Library Cataloguing-in-Publication
Data: A catalogue record for this book is
available from the British Library

Conceived, designed and produced by
Quarto Publishing plc
The Old Brewery
6 Blundell Street
London N7 9BH

QUAR.UUDL

Project editor Vicky Weber
Art editor Karla Jennings
Assistant art director Penny Cobb
Designer James Lawrence
Copy editor Sarah Hoggett
Proofreader Gillian Kemp
Indexer Diana Le Core

Art director Moira Clinch
Publisher Piers Spence

Manufactured by
Universal Graphics Pte Ltd., Singapore
Printed by
Leefung-Asco Printers Ltd, China

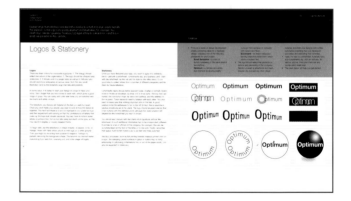

Contents

Introduction

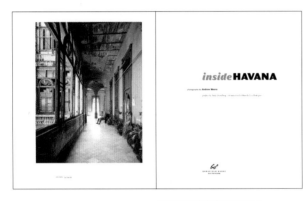

The purpose of this book is to give an overview of the graphic design process. It is intended for both beginners, who can gain an insight into what is involved in creating effective designs, and more experienced designers who may want a refresher course or new design ideas and approaches.

The book is divided into two sections. The first, Basic Design Principles, concerns the fundamentals of design – the choices designers have to make about typeface, colour, composition, illustrations, photographs and so on. The second section, Design Projects and Categories, looks at specific areas of design, such as logotypes, magazines, brochures, advertisements and web design, and at the considerations specific to each one. In both sections, each topic is comprised of a short explanation illustrated by examples of good professional practice and practical exercises for you to try.

Throughout the book, you are encouraged to analyse your work. Being able to assess what you do and be objective about it is an essential part of the learning process: it not only allows you to develop as a designer, but also makes you more aware of the questions that need to be asked (and answered) in any design project. You also need to be able to accept criticism of your work and to view it in a positive way. If you work in isolation, without any regard for other people's opinions, then you run the risk of becoming too rigid in your approach. However, any comments on a design should always be directed towards trying to improve it. Negative comments such as 'I don't like this', without a constructive suggestion for improvement, hinder the design process and can ultimately block your development.

For the purposes of this book, it is assumed that you will already have the computer skills and facilities needed for the practical exercises. You will need to have access to common software packages.

How to use this book

Section 1

The first few paragraphs give a theoretical overview of the subject in hand – in this case 'Display Typefaces'. Beneath this summary, you will find 'Design decisions'. These are captions that explain the thumbnail pictures on the rest of the double-page spread.

These specially commissioned artworks illustrate and clarify the design theory being examined. Each one is numbered and corresponds to an explanatory sentence in the 'Design decisions'.

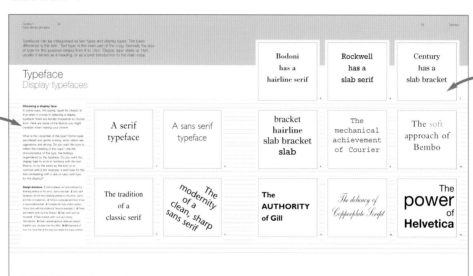

In each section there are exercises that encourage you to practise the design theory on the preceding pages.

Professional examples to give you inspiration! Look at how a range of experienced designers from around the world have approached the points covered in each subject.

Example answers are given in illustrations accompanying each of the exercises.

Section 2

This introduction to each project includes common good practice techniques and hints on how to achieve a professional look in your design.

Try your hand at creative design in this open exercise – you are given instructions about what to produce, then it's up to you! Sample designs give you a few ideas to get started, but it's your challenge to create your own design innovations. Don't forget to show your work to friends and colleagues – their opinions and constructive advice will speed on your progress.

One professional example is studied in some depth. Breaking down the design and reviewing its individual components helps you to understand how and why the designer constructed the piece in this way.

Examples from around the world illustrate a range of professional designers' approaches to each design category.

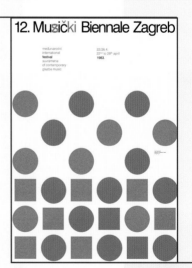

Section One

Basic Design Principles

This section explains and illustrates the various components of the design process – the 'building blocks' of every basic composition – for example, using images, selecting a typeface and combining image and type. This will make the process of design accessible to you, as long as you are willing to spend some time studying and exploring each facet in close detail.

Each component provides a short summary of the subject, followed by visual examples. There then follows a practical exercise and examples of work by professional designers showing how they have approached the basic design principle in question. By looking at these examples, you can see the decision-making process in action.

One of the first points to consider is the shape and size of your design.
Getting the proportion of length to width right is crucial so that your design
comfortably and stylishly fits the space available.

Basic Shapes
Shaping and forming

Factors involved:

The format of a project is more often than not predetermined to accommodate both the desired end result and the design function.

When choosing the format of a design for print, practical considerations, such as paper shapes and sizes and the flexibility of the printing presses available, are your guide – always make sure you find out what parameters you are working within and what you need to achieve. If, for example, the client will need to post the layout, there is no point creating a fantastic design that will not fit in any envelope.

There are also some financial factors that govern format. Unusually curved cuts or impractical shapes are expensive to produce; similarly the uneconomic division of paper sizes can be expensive since it causes unnecessary waste.

When you have dealt with the more mundane factors, you can start to think about the aesthetic feel of the design. You do not want to use a shape that causes you to lose information, nor do you want one that leaves a lot of empty space.

If you use photographs or illustrations, the pictorial content should be your guide – text can easily run around the images. If you are dealing with text alone, this might lead

naturally to a particular format – for instance, novels are nearly always portrait as the eye tires quickly when reading block text set in lines longer than ten to twelve words. The priority here is to ensure that the shape does not inhibit understanding.

Similar considerations apply when you turn your attention to the shape of the individual components of the design. Think logically about what you want to achieve, for it is shapes that provide the basis for the feel and style of any design – for example, a teen magazine should have a lot of exciting shapes and can afford to be quite busy, while a sophisticated designer label might be composed of one simple, small shape in an expanse of space.

Design decisions 1 A billboard poster must fit the size of the hoarding. **2** A formal document tends to focus on content rather than design, so neither the format nor the shape of the contents should be fashioned to catch attention. **3** The format of packaging is dictated by the need to fit the product. **4** A flyer gets handed out on the street – a remarkable basic shape will make it more memorable. **5** First impressions count – the format adds to the message. **6** Supermarket publicity brochures need to fit in customers' bags but contain a lot of information – a rectangular shape that folds small is perfect. It is important to ensure elements of the design are not ruined by falling on the folds. **7** Shapes of pictures can be determined by the shape of the subject – text fits around the images. **8** A vertical format is required as the tall, thin image would be lost on a horizontal form.

Escape from the city
Balloon tours

1

2

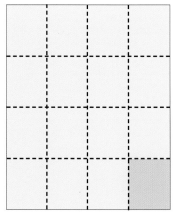

3

4

Building for Success

The Sky is the Limit

5

6

7

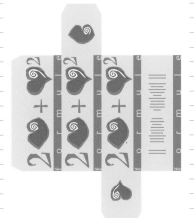

Places of Culture

Design an exhibition brochure for a local photographic society. Design three black-and-white double-page spreads, using at least eight photographs over the three spreads.

8

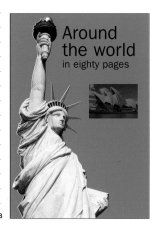

Around the world in eighty pages

Exercise 1

- Find a photograph that contains a lot of interest and detail.
- Scan the photograph and select the format that you consider best suits the subject matter.
- Now take the same photograph and try cropping in an alternative format.
- Finally, crop in on some of the interesting parts of the image. Comment on what you see.

Exercise 2

- Find a poem, a recipe or a set of instructions.
- Typeset one of these pieces of copy in 11pt and place it in an A5 format.
- Add features to improve the clarity of the text.
- Now experiment with a variety of formats and shapes.
- Print out your work and assess the different versions.

1

ILENE PERLMAN
PHOTOGRAPHER

1 **A portrait format provided the perfect space for this
cropped image.**
2 **The landscape format allows the design to consist of
two wide photographs plus a narrow one in this
promotional card for a photographer.**

2

CHERRY PIE

Makes 1 pie

Ingredients
2 cups all-purpose flour
1 cup shortening
1/2 cup cold water
1 pinch salt
2 cups pitted sour cherries
1 1/4 cups white sugar
10 teaspoons cornstarch
1 tablespoon butter
1/4 teaspoon almond extract

Directions
1   Cut the shortening into the flour and salt with the whisking blades of a
    stand mixer until the crumbs are pea sized. Mix in cold war. Refrigerate
    until chilled through. Roll out dough for a two crust pie. Line a 9 inch pie
    pan with pastry.

2   Place the cherries, sugar, and cornstarch in a medium size non-aluminum
    saucepan. Allow the mixture to stand for 10 minutes, or until the cherries
    are moistened with the sugar. Bring to a boil over medium heat, stirring
    constantly. Lower the heat; simmer for 1 minute, or until the juices thicken
    and become translucent. Remove pan from heat, and stir in butter and
    almond extract. Pour the filling into the pie shell. Cover with top crust.

3   Bake in a preheated 375° F (190° C) oven for 45 to 55 minutes,
    or until the crust is golden brown.

CHERRY PIE

Makes 1 pie

Directions

1   Cut the shortening into the flour and salt with the whisking blades
    of a stand mixer until the crumbs are pea sized. Mix in cold war.
    Refrigerate until chilled through. Roll out dough for a two crust
    pie. Line a 9 inch pie pan with pastry.

2   Place the cherries, sugar, and cornstarch in a medium size
    non-aluminum saucepan. Allow the mixture to stand for 10 minutes,
    or until the cherries are moistened with the sugar. Bring to a boil
    over medium heat, stirring constantly. Lower the heat; simmer for 1
    minute, or until the juices thicken and become translucent. Remove
    pan from heat, and stir in butter and almond extract. Pour the filling
    into the pie shell. Cover with top crust.

3   Bake in a preheated 375° F (190° C) oven for 45 to 55 minutes,
    or until the crust is golden brown.

Ingredients
2 cups all-purpose flour
1 cup shortening
1/2 cup cold water
1 pinch salt
2 cups pitted sour cherries
1 1/4 cups white sugar
10 teaspoons cornstarch
1 tablespoon butter
1/4 teaspoon almond extract

Exercise 3

- Draw 10 to 15 shapes on a pad of paper and cut them out. The shapes can be turned on their side and have portions removed or added.
- Experiment with these shapes by cutting them out of various attractive materials – coloured paper, shiny or matt surfaces, newspaper or magazines, even odd scraps of fabric.
- Mount them on a large piece of card and rate them in order of attractiveness. Alongside each one, write a brief comment on its aesthetic values.

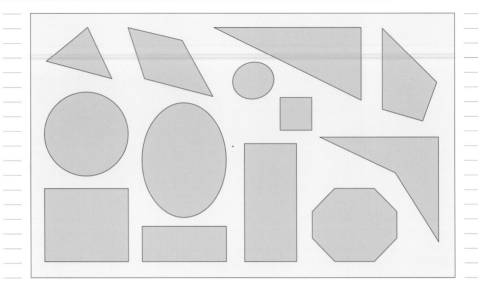

Exercise 4

- Look at the following list of words and produce, either on the computer or by hand, shapes that you feel evoke the meaning of each word: harsh, soft, strong, weak, ugly, boring, regular, exciting, mundane, flowing, complicated, sophisticated.
- When you have completed this, do the opposite – select shapes that are opposite to the feeling of the words.
- Finally, compare the two exercises. The first should be pleasing to you, while the second should seem incongruous and not quite right.

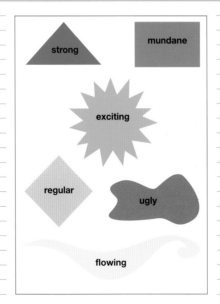

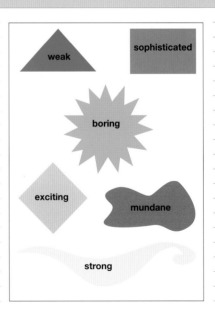

1

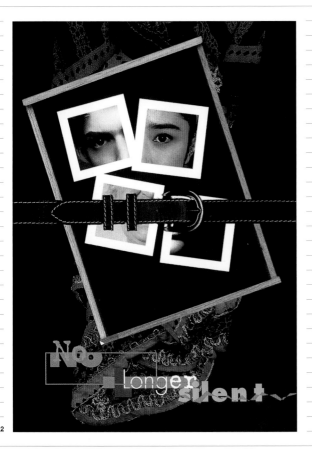

2

3

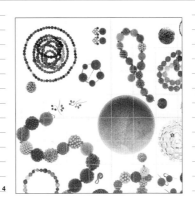

4

1 The landscape format gives a lot of scope for interesting text and image shapes. So as to avoid placing any part of the design over the paper folds, the composition utilises a variety of text lengths and picture sizes. The result is a visually exciting but ultimately clear and accessible design.

2 The way the pictures have been cropped and text has been shaped forms the basis for the dramatic feel of this design.

3 The close-up of the facial features along with the torn-paper effect create a powerful and haunting composition.

4 A sheet of stamps printed with randomly placed items of jewellery – this is a promotional teaser campaign to encourage the creative use of individual stamps.

All good design should show a balance between its different elements.
This balance should create a sense of harmony, so that the reader is visually
attracted to the design and is also able to understand the meaning.

Basic shapes
Placing a single word or heading

Using space to its full potential
The exact placement of all elements in any
design is critical to establish balance and
harmony. In this first exercise we will look at
various ways of placing a single word on a
page to see how the relationship between
that word and the space around it can evoke
different moods.

There are various ways of positioning type on
a page: it can be ranged left (in other words,
with each line left aligned), ranged right or
centred. You can also change the direction of
type from horizontal to vertical, set type at an
angle and even break away from the convention
of setting it in a straight line parallel to the edge
of the page.

Design decisions 1 The type is centred and placed just
above the midline, creating an even appearance.
2 The type may be moved nearer the top – but how
close? **3** Type touching the top edge creates an unusual
effect, but balance must be supplied by other elements in
the design. **4** Or it may be placed at the bottom. **5** Type
may be enlarged to full page width. **6** Or made larger.
7 Or made smaller. **8** Positioning type near the edge of
the page increases tension. **9** As does a change in
direction. **10** A different angle can be hard to read, but
creates a visual contrast. **11** The type may be run around
the top of a semicircle. **12** Or around the bottom of a
semicircle. **13** Or it can follow a curve. All of the last
three have the advantage of dynamism at the expense
of some readability.

MASTHEAD

5

MAST
HEAD

6

MASTHEAD

7

MASTHEAD

8

MASTHEAD

9

MASTHEAD

10

MASTHEAD

11

MASTHEAD

12

MASTHEAD

13

Exercise 5

- Select an A6 landscape format.
- Typeset one word of at least seven letters in upper and lower case in a type size appropriate to the working area.
- Position the word in the space available in a central position.
- Create three design variations: i range left; ii display vertically; iii display at an angle of 45°.
- Now try positioning the word around a semicircle.
- And increase the tracking.
- Look at all these variations and decide what mood they evoke.

Exercise 6

- Select an A4 format.
- Choose a word of at least seven letters and reverse it out of a black background in upper and lower case.
- Use a sans serif typeface as it will be more legible in a reverse-out situation.
- Experiment with various type sizes and tracking widths.
- Divide the format in half, make one half white and the other black, and position the heading in one or other of the halves.
- When you have completed all four variations, analyse their effects. Revise the examples according to your critical analysis.

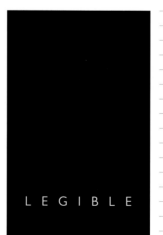

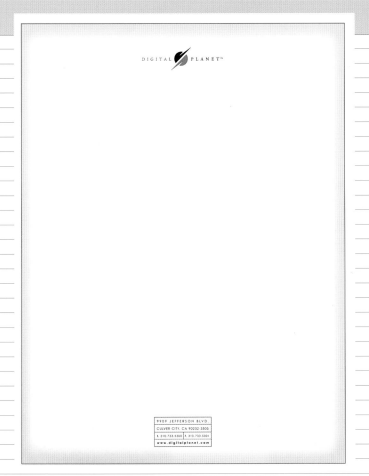

1

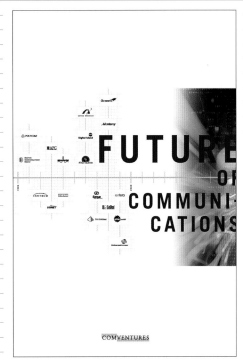

2

1 **The heading and contact details
  are centred to complement the
  symmetrical shape of the symbol.**
2 **A futuristic feel is achieved by
  setting the copy range right and
  on the far edge of the page.**
3 **The imaginative use of
  contrasting vertical and
  horizontal settings is perfect for
  the precise, technical approach of
  an architectural organisation.**
4 **The interesting way this main
  heading has been cut in two
  increases the visual presentation
  without sacrificing any legibility.**

4

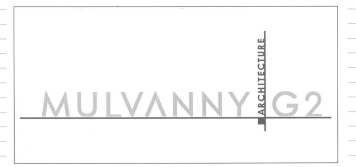

3

When you combine a heading with an image or block of text, the heading not only has to relate to the format of the page, but must also harmonise with the other elements if the design is to achieve the desired effect.

Basic shapes
Combining a heading with an image or block of text

Using various elements to create harmony
One advantage of having more elements is that you also have more options: you can alter the size, angle and direction of the different elements to make them balance with each other on the page.

Visually it is better to have unequal proportions, with the heading either much larger than the picture, so that it dominates it, or much smaller, so that the picture is more prominent than the text. The question you have to ask yourself is whether the heading or the image is the most important element.

Design decisions Both heading and text can be set in the same typeface but in different sizes or weights in either **1** Symmetrical style or **2** Asymmetrical style. **3** Alternatively, give different degrees of emphasis. The actual content of the picture will influence which option to go for. Here the heading dominates. **4** Here the picture dominates. **5** Most drama ensues when the proportions of picture to text are unequal. **6** Visually it is more interesting to integrate the heading and text. **7** Having the heading running in a different direction to the text adds variety to a layout. **8** The text can be set so that it echoes the shape of the picture.

Typefaces

The ever-increasing flexibility of computer typesetting equipment with the ability to set a wide range of point sizes has done much to popularise the trend towards the use of typeface families. These are typefaces available in a range of weights and derivatives. Many new typefaces now have a semi-bold version that offers the designer a useful choice of weight between the regular and bold designs.

1

Typeface availability

The ever-increasing flexibility of computer typesetting equipment with the ability to set a wide range of point sizes has done much to popularise the trend towards the use of typeface families. These are typefaces available in a range of weights and derivatives. Many new typefaces now have a semi-bold version that offers the designer a useful choice of weight between the regular and bold designs.

2

TYPEFACES

Typefaces

The ever-increasing flexibility of computer typesetting equipment with the ability to set a wide range of point sizes has done much to popularise the trend towards the use of typeface families. These are typefaces available in a range of weights and derivatives. Many new typefaces now have a semi-bold version that offers the designer a useful choice of weight between the regular and bold designs.

3

6

Typefaces

Typefaces

The ever-increasing flexibility of computer typesetting equipment with the ability to set a wide range of point sizes has done much to popularise the trend towards the use of typeface families. These are typefaces available in a range of weights and derivatives. Many new typefaces now have a semi-bold version that offers the designer a useful choice of weight between the regular and bold designs.

4

7

Typefaces

The ever-increasing flexibility of computer typesetting equipment with the ability to set a wide range of point sizes has done much to popularise the trend towards the use of typeface families.

5

Typefaces

The ever-increasing flexibility of computer typesetting equipment with the ability to set a wide range of point sizes has done much to popularise the trend towards the use of typeface families.

8

Exercise 7

- From a newspaper or magazine, cut out a small article that has a heading and text of at least 50–70 words. Working to an A5 portrait format and using a serif typeface, set the copy justified with the heading centred over the text.
- Now change the typeface for the heading to a bold sans serif typeface and set the text ranged left unjustified. The arrangement should be off-centred within the format.
- Experiment with the size of the heading and its placement in relation to the text. You could place the heading so that it interrupts the text or is in more extreme conflict with it. Don't be afraid to try out new things.

Lee Konitz

Associated with 'The birth of the cool', Lee Konitz came from Chicago and has been playing alto sax for over five decades. He is now 75 and has made hundreds of albums, mainly with small record companies. What marks out his career is that he declined early on to be yet another Charlie Parker clone; he has remained an exploratory, innovative saxophonist.

Lee Konitz

Associated with 'The birth of the cool', Lee Konitz came from Chicago and has been playing alto sax for over five decades. He is now 75 and has made hundreds of albums, mainly with small record companies. What marks out his career is that he declined early on to be yet another Charlie Parker clone; he has remained an exploratory, innovative saxophonist.

Lee Konitz
Associated with 'The birth of the cool', Lee Konitz came from Chicago and has been playing alto sax for over five decades. He is now 75 and has made hundreds of albums, mainly with small record companies. What marks out his career is that he declined early on to be yet another Charlie Parker clone; he has remained an exploratory, innovative saxophonist.

Lee Konitz

Associated with 'The birth of the cool', Lee Konitz came from Chicago and has been playing alto sax for over five decades. He is now 75 and has made hundreds of albums, mainly with small record companies. What marks out his career is that he declined early on to be yet another Charlie Parker clone; he has remained an exploratory, innovative saxophonist.

Exercise 8

- Find a suitable photograph and set it with some text. The photograph should occupy 80 percent of the area.
- Now reverse this ratio, so that the picture occupies 20 per cent and the text and white space take up 80 per cent. Also experiment by changing the angle of the text and picture.
- Lastly, select your own proportions of text to picture and composition.
- When you have completed the exercises, analyse their effect and comment on each one. Revise the examples according to your own critical analysis.

Combining a heading with an image or block of text

two magpies = 雙喜 double   happiness (*shuāng xǐ*)

嘉鵲。人們祝富雙喜「先秦時代，人們認為喜鵲
具有應拓心之喜事本息，可以圖片形式的到來
一隻喜鵲相向並頭立，傳述報喜之畫。客人喜臨
即「嘉鵲為福之福畫。因「雙喜，兩隻喜鵲一相
逢，一象徵滿滿好音的觀兆，即「雙喜，一相
連、一圖畫祝福分向半，「雙」的禮意「雙喜」
傳說如鏡子分向半，「雙夫妻在家和人心
磁、面如鏡半分向半，一人持半「如夫妻分向
傳說子分向半，一人持半」如夫妻在家和人心
、人常常才看圖鵲素報顏蒂的有情。

magpie / The characters for 'magpie,' *xǐ que*, literally mean the 'bird of happiness.' A picture of two magpies facing each other stands for 'double happiness,' *shuāng xǐ*, symbolic of conjugal bliss. The call of a magpie foretells the arrival of a guest, good news, or good fortune. A magpie resting on a plum branch conveys the wish 'happiness before one's brow,' *xǐ shàng méi shāo*, as the word for 'plum' and 'brow'

are both pronounced *méi*. Magpies also served to preserve the integrity of a marriage, according to legend. When a husband and wife were to be apart for any reason, they would break a mirror and each take half. If the wife was unfaithful, her half of the mirror turned into a magpie that flew back and informed her husband. Consequently, an image of a magpie is often placed on the back of a mirror.

double happiness ⑧ **171**

1

1 This design successfully overcomes the difficult problem of combining two very different languages. Their positioning allows them both to be read easily and without conflict.

2 The use of colour in the heading means it can be overprinted onto the text, creating a strong visual impact.

Il y en a que j'aime plus que d'autres. Les gens ne les comprennent pas tous de la même façon: quand ils les découvrent, je les découvre. Je suis étonné et bouleversé quand, parfois, j'en emmène un au format gigantesque de l'affiche.
Leur petite taille, pratique et humble, impose une grande précision dans la narration, par le mot, ou l'image : une gymnastique que j'adore, celle du raccourci.
Il y a des "collectors", des "petits coupons" qui ont existé et que j'ai supprimé par manque de conviction. D'autres que j'ai réimprimé, avec des corrections.
Il y a des collectionneurs. Il y a eu des articles dans les journaux sur ces petites images. Il y en a du se promenant à Paris, à Londres, ou à New York.

Cette exposition s'appella "Super !".
Le "SUPER !"-VERNISSAGE a eu lieu le 26 mai 00. L'exposition dure jusqu'au 29 septembre 00, et sera peut être remont(r)ée à Paris.
D'ordinaire données, ces petites images seront vendues 1 F pièce pendant toute la durée de l'exposition, dans le "SUPER !"-MARCHÉ.

Cinq premiers "petits coupons" créés en 1994.
La "collection" en compte aujourd'hui, une centaine.
Cent prochains sont à l'état de notes, et je suis aujourd'hui certain d'avoir le profond désir d'en créer de nouveaux, toute ma vie durant.

2

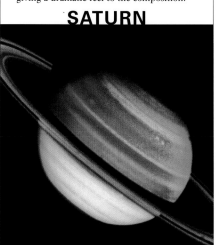

The image, size and interesting cropping ensure that the image dominates the text, giving a dramatic feel to the composition.

SATURN

Saturn

Drastically reducing the image size and including more text gives the design a much more informative feel and encourages the reader to delve into the story and use the image as little more than a visual reference.

Saturn

Here, the image size has been increased to occupy a third of the area, but the emphasis is still on the text. The image has been cropped and much of the detail has been lost. In situations where the information contained in the image is not of critical importance, this is a useful way of pulling the reader into the article.

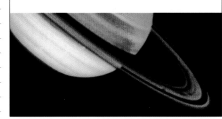

Within a single design, you might have to deal with a number of different elements, such as a two- or three-line heading, a subheading, main text and pictures to accompany that text. The more elements you have to consider, the more difficult it is to achieve harmony.

Balance and harmony
Combining and positioning multiple elements

Engaging multiple elements
The first step is to decide on the relative importance of each element and how much emphasis you need to give to each one. Start by selecting a typeface, size and weight for the heading. Then go through the same procedure for any subheadings and the text.

With the main text, you also have to decide on the type measure. How many columns should it occupy? How will the heading relate to the number of columns? Will the pictures fit into the column widths or will they look too cramped or too spacious? Try out various combinations before you make your final choice.

Design decisions 1 A symmetrical arrangement. The text and picture have equal emphasis, and the heading is centred over both. The result is a quiet harmony. **2** An asymmetrical arrangement, with less text than in the first example and the emphasis on the picture. **3** The heading dominates. **4** The picture dominates. **5** The picture still dominates but is in a different format. **6** The heading runs in a different direction to the text. **7** Change of shape, with heading, subheading, text and picture integrated. **8** Multiple columns, with space giving emphasis to the headings.

Heading

Here, text and image take up equal amounts of space. The shape of the image allows more background detail to be included, thus reducing the emphasis on the main subject, the balloon. Justifying the text and centring both image and text gives the design a rather static appearance. The overall composition is gentle in feel.

1

Heading

In this example the image has much more impact, even though the image and text have the same proportions as in the first example. The reason for this is that the background detail has been reduced, drawing attention much more quickly to the balloon. The text is ranged left and the overall appearance has more drama than the one above.

2

HEADING

This approach uses a strong display heading to catch the reader's eye before he or she moves on to the image and text. The size of the heading in bold capitals ensures that it dominates the design. The other elements in the arrangement have been reduced to the point where they become almost insignificant.

3

The image has been removed completely, and so the reader has to be attracted into the subject by the display heading. The heading could be set very large or, if space is tight, given extra emphasis by being placed in vertically. In this example, there are four text columns. With columns this narrow, it is better to range the type left to avoid excessive word spacing and word breaks. If there is sufficient copy, you could introduce some subheadings. These can be set in a bold version of the typeface.

Heading

6

Heading

Here the image size is enlarged to occupy two-thirds of the format, giving a change of emphasis. This has a similar effect to that shown in the second example, in that the image is the main attraction and text is pushed into the background.

4

Heading

Subhead Here there is a change of direction of image, heading and text. By slicing away parts of the image, the reflection of the balloon has gone. This arrangement is much more dynamic, but the text is less readable and there is not nearly as much information in the image.

7

Heading

The emphasis here remains on the image, although text and image occupy more or less the same amount of space. Cropping the image and concentrating upon the balloon quickly attracts the eye to the subject. This treatment means losing background detail.

5

Heading 1

This example gives the best of both worlds. The image attracts attention; at the same time, the three columns with their separate headings give

Heading 2

added visual interest. This type of composition can be flexible if the copy is limited; as a variation, you could remove one of the columns

Heading 3

and increase the image size or the column measure. As in example 7, range the text left without any word breaks.

8

Exercise 9

- Using the same format and style as in exercise 8, place the text and photograph alongside each other with the heading centred above them.
- Now change this so that the photograph dominates the space and the text and heading are off-centred.

Equal Proportions

The image size and the text have equal emphasis. 'Bleeding off' the image into the left-hand edge gives the design added visual impact.

The problem here is that a lot of the image area has now been lost, and so its informational value is diminished.

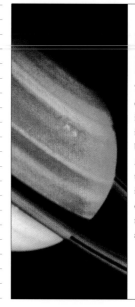

Larger Image

This arrangement has even more drama. The image size has been increased and now bleeds off on two sides. Again, the problem is the information that is lost as the image is decreased further: the rings of the planet have almost disappeared.

Exercise 10

- Using the same material as in exercise 9, change the photograph so that it is long and thin. Add additional text to the original and place the heading at a different angle.
- Lastly, cut out a photograph in a circular shape and set the text so that it integrates with the image.
- When you have completed the exercises, analyse their effect and comment on each one. Return to the examples and revise them according to your critical analysis.

Abstraction is Nearer

Visually, this looks more interesting because the proportions of the two elements are unequal. An added visual trick is that the heading runs at an angle. By restricting the image to a small area, it becomes more abstract – but the amount of information in the image has been dramatically reduced.

Circular Shapes

Although the image shape looks good, it has no informational value whatsoever and has become pure abstraction. This is acceptable if shape alone is the criteria for the design. The circular shape invites a text to be set around it, which gives a good structure to the composition. In this type of arrangement, the text should be ranged left; this avoids the kind of exaggerated word spaces that would be produced with justified setting.

Combining and positioning multiple elements

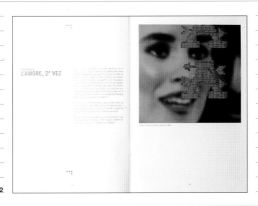

1

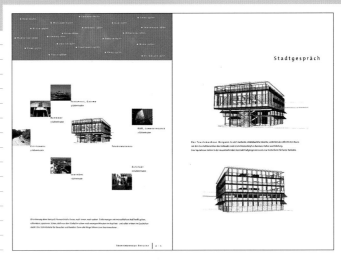

4

2

5

3

1 The vertical heading combines well with the landscape images, allowing them maximum width.

2 Image and text are aligned at the foot; this combined with a generous use of space gives a good balance and a modern feel to the design.

3 The positioning of the heading and subheading over two lines fits comfortably with the image style.

4 The apparently random manner in which each image and caption is set creates tension and increases the visual interest of this stylish design.

5 Using circular shapes is quite an unusual approach; the text has been set to match the curves, creating an eye-catching, harmonised design.

A grid divides the page into blocks of space, or units. These units act as a guide for positioning the text, pictures and captions on your layout. The grid is an 'organiser'. It is a great help in getting things in a logical order and is an essential tool when a team of designers are working together on a project.

Balance and harmony
The use of the grid

The content will determine the grid

The number of units within the grid depends on the complexity of the material you are working with. The more involved the content, the more versatile the grid needs to be.

A simple grid might have equal divisions, with maybe three divisions horizontally and vertically.

A more complex grid might vary in unit size and also have far more divisions so that it can accommodate both copy that varies in length and importance and pictures of varying sizes.

Design decisions The grid will show the margins around the area. There should also be a channel of space between the units. **1** A simple grid with nine units. Note the space for margins at the top (head), bottom (foot) and sides. When constructing a grid, use hairline rules for the internal divisions and 1pt rules for the outer lines. **2** Information should start at the top left of a unit, as in these examples. **3** When devising your grid, it is important to show a double-page spread. The reason for this is that you always view a spread when reading. **4** A photograph should occupy whole units of the grid. **5** Photographs can occupy more than one unit – 1 x 1, 1 x 3, 2 x 2, 3 x 3, for example. **6** A more complex grid, with more units and unequal proportions.
7 Narrow units can be used to accommodate captions to the photographs.

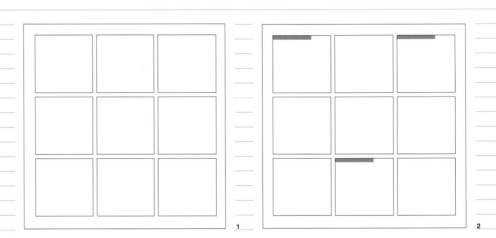

1   2

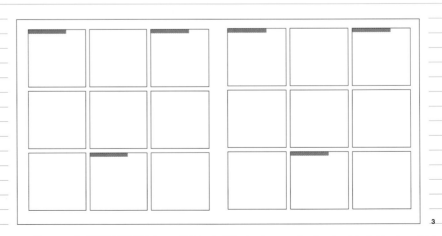

3

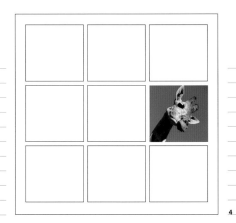

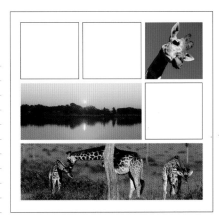

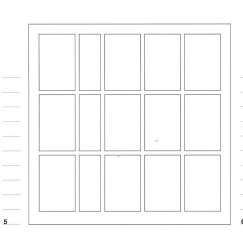

4

5

6

7

Exercise 11

- Using a landscape A5 format, divide the space equally into three parts, both vertically and horizontally, with 6-mm (¼-in) margins.
- Using this grid, typeset copy in a 10pt sans serif typeface so at least five of the units are used. Add a heading. Make sure you place the copy to the top left of the units.
- Try this in several positions on the grid.

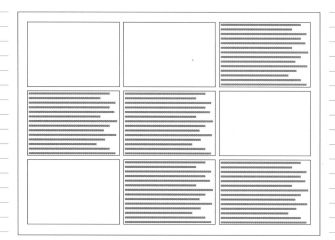

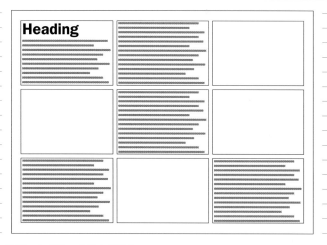

Heading

Exercise 12

- Change the format to A4 square and construct a grid with four equal horizontal divisions and five vertical ones. One of the vertical divisions should be half the width of the other four.
- Select some text from a magazine and set it in 9pt type with 2pt leading, ranged left. The total amount of text should not exceed one grid unit.
- Now choose three photographs and, using the same heading as in exercise 11, try out several compositions, varying the size of the photographs, the measure of the text and the number of grid units covered. When you change the measure of the text, remember to keep to the dimensions of the grid units.

Heading

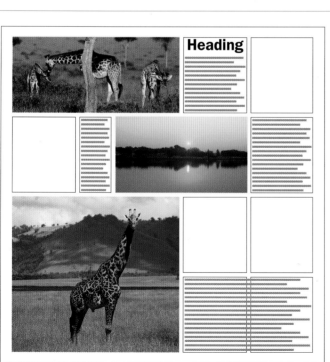

Heading

inside **HAVANA**

1 This title page shows good
use of the grid with simple,
uncomplicated vertical and
horizontal alignments.

2–3 These spreads
demonstrate how flexible a
grid can be. The text is set
in variable measures while
the captions are a single
unit width. The effect is
busy, vibrant and exciting.

Typefaces can be categorised as text types and display types. The basic difference is the size. 'Text type' is the main part of the copy. Normally the size of type for this purpose ranges from 8 to 12pt. 'Display type' starts at 14pt; usually it serves as a heading, or as a brief introduction to the main copy.

Typeface
Display typefaces

Choosing a display face

In some ways, the saying 'spoilt for choice' is true when it comes to selecting a display typeface: there are literally thousands to choose from. Here are some of the factors you might consider when making your choice:

What is the visual feel of the type? Some types are refined and gentle looking, while others are aggressive and strong. Do you want the type to reflect the meaning of the copy? Use the characteristics of the type, the feelings engendered by the typeface. Do you want the display type to work in harmony with the text (that is, to be the same as the text) or to contrast with it (for example, a serif type for the text contrasting with a slab or sans serif type for the display)?

Design decisions   1 Serif typefaces are characterised by finishing strokes on the arms, stems and tails. **2** Sans serif typefaces do not have finishing strokes on the arms, stems and tails of characters. **3** Times is a popular serif font; it has a very traditional feel. **4** Compare the look of this modern Stone Sans with the traditional Times in example 3. **5** There are hairline serifs such as Bodoni. **6** Slab serifs such as Rockwell. **7** Slab bracket serifs such as Century Schoolbook. **8** When several typeface styles are placed together, you can see how they differ. **9–13** Examples of how the visual feel of the type can reflect the copy content.

A serif typeface

1

A sans serif typeface

2

The tradition of a classic serif

3

The modernity of a clean, sharp sans serif

4

Bodoni
has a
hairline serif

5

Rockwell
has a
slab serif

6

Century
has a
slab bracket

7

bracket
hairline
slab bracket
slab

8

The
mechanical
achievement
of Courier

9

The soft
approach of
Bembo

10

The
AUTHORITY
of Gill

11

The delicacy of
Copperplate Script

12

The
power
of
Helvetica

13

Exercise 13

- Select a portrait A4 format
  and set the following pieces of
  copy in a display typeface that
  you feel is appropriate to the
  meaning of the words, in
  either upper and lower case or
  all capitals:
  - pure poetry
  - traces of conflict
  - keep off the grass
  - down memory lane

pure poetry

traces of
conflict

**KEEP OFF
THE GRASS**

Down Memory Lane

Exercise 14

- This time, work the other way
  round and let the typeface
  lead. Using the following
  typefaces, write copy that
  reflects the feel of each one:
  - Bembo italic
  - Helvetica bold
  - Rockwell light

*Hand crafted
porcelain since 1851.*

**You will find a lifejacket
located underneath
your seat.**

October 18, 23.00 pm.
Suspect enters side
entrance. Visibility is poor.

1

1 The rough, handmade stencil typeform combines extremely
  well with the image.
2 Clever manipulation of the type through changes in size,
  alignment and position fit perfectly with the sense of the
  words. The closeness of the letters also creates tension.
3 The type has been imaginatively treated to mimic the feel of
  the movement of dance.
4 The use of a sans serif, extended typeface in such a large
  size gives the design an expansive look and reflects the
  meaning of the words.

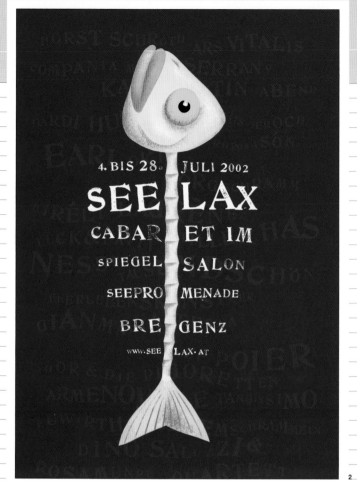

2

3

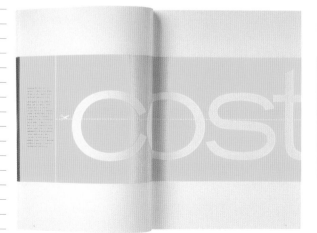

4

There are certain typefaces that can be termed 'classic' typefaces. These are text typefaces that have stood the test of time and remain in popular use because of their inherent quality in form and aesthetic structure.

Typeface
Text and typefaces

Types for text setting

Types such as Bembo, Garamond, Caslon, Times, Palatino and Plantin are examples of classics that, when used with other criteria, such as a realistic size, will almost guarantee a readable piece of text.

The things to consider when selecting a text type are similar to those for selecting a display face, but there is one added priority: function. In other words, what is the purpose of the text? Will it be read continuously, like a novel? Will the text be broken up with subheadings, so that readers can access small pieces of information easily? Or is the overall look more important than what's actually being said?

In selecting your text type, consider this:
• The x-height of the typeface.
• The set, or overall width, of the typeface.
• The visual feel of the type; this can reflect and enhance the meaning of the copy.

Design decisions 1 The x-height is the height of the body of the typeface (it takes its name from the lower case x). The ascender is any part of a lowercase character that lies above the x-height (for example, the arm of the 'b'). The descender is any part of a character that falls below the x-height (for example, the stem of the 'p'). **2** Typefaces with small x-heights, such as Bembo, look smaller than typefaces with larger x-heights, such as Times New Roman, in the same point size. **3** Wide-set typefaces such as Century

Schoolbook require wider measures than typefaces with a narrow set, such as Ehrhardt. **4–6** Instructional text: orders or warnings are better set in sans serif typefaces, which look more authoritative than classic serif typefaces or italics. **7** Continuous running text: the classic typefaces discussed above are the best choice. The optimum number of words is 10–12 words per line. **8** Factual texts: these texts still need to be read continuously, but there are pauses, with prominent headings and subheadings. A sans serif typeface could be used here, giving you the added advantage of well designed and related heading weights. **9–11** Magazine work: the priority here is not so much readability, but style. Style magazines, in particular, tend to be more adventurous. The classic typefaces can look too gentle. Typefaces such as Erhardt, Stone and Rotis are popular.

The body is the x-height

The peak is the ascender

The trough is the descender

1

Bembo has a small x-height

Times has a large x-height

2

The set width differs

The set width differs

3

**Keep off
the grass**

Keep off
the grass

*Keep off
the grass*

4

5

6

Mackintosh's influence on the avant-garde abroad was great, especially in Germany and Austria, so much so that the advanced style of the early 20th century was sometimes known as 'Mackintoshismus'. His work was exhibited in Budapest, Munich, Dresden, Venice and Moscow, arousing interest and excitement everywhere. From 1914 he lived in London and Port Vendres. Thereafter, apart from a house in Northampton, none of his major architectural projects reached the stage of execution, although he did complete some work as a designer of fabrics, book covers, furniture and painted watercolours.

7

Helvetica
Ubiquitous sans serif typeface designed by Max Meidinger and Edouard Hoffman and issued by the Swiss typefoundry, Hass, in 1957.

Origin
It is based on Akzidenz Grotesque, an alphabet popular at the turn of the century.

8

Ehrhardt
This typeface is based on originals from the Ehrhardt foundry from Leipzig in the early eighteenth century. An elegant serif typeface similar to Jenson, it has a narrow set width that allows more characters to the line, making it ideal for magazine work.

9

Stone Sans
This versatile sans serif was designed by Sumner Stone in 1987 to meet the requirements of low-resolution laser printing. There are three weights available – medium, semi-bold and bold. The face harmonises with Stone Serif and Stone Informal.

10

Rotis Semi-Sans
A popular sans serif throughout the 1990s, Rotis Semi-Sans was designed by Otl Aicher in 1989. Condensed in structure, some characters exhibit variations in the thickness of the strokes. It is available in four weights – light, regular, medium and bold.

11

Exercise 15

- Select a measure of about 10cm (4 in). Type out any piece of copy so that you have at least four lines, and then set it in 4, 8, 12 and 16pt Sabon. Decide which size looks best in the given measure.
- Take this preferred size and set it in Century Schoolbook (a wide-set typeface), then repeat the exercise using a narrow-set typeface such as Ehrhardt.
- Look at the two together and compare the results.

There are many factors to consider when thinking about readability and legibility of the text. These include the line length (measure), the size of type, the weight of type, the amount of leading and the size of the x-height.

4pt

There are many factors to consider when thinking about readability and legibility of the text. These include the line length (measure), the size of type, the weight of type, the amount of leading and the size of the x-height.

8pt

There are many factors to consider when thinking about readability and legibility of the text. These include the line length (measure), the size of type, the weight of type, the amount of leading and the size of the x-height.

10pt

There are many factors to consider when thinking about readability and legibility of the text. These include the line length (measure), the size of type, the weight of type, the amount of leading and the size of the x-height.

12pt

There are many factors to consider when thinking about readability and legibility of the text. These include the line length (measure), the size of type, the weight of type, the amount of leading and the size of the x-height.

16pt

Exercise 16

- Typeset the copy 'The apparent size of a typeface varies according to the x-height.' in 12pt Bembo.
- Repeat in Times New Roman
- Look at the two together and compare the results.

The apparent size of a typeface varies according to the x-height.

The apparent size of a typeface varies according to the x-height.

[X I N E T]

VERSATILE

WebNative and

WebNative Venture allow users to access the

FullPress server over the Internet. Regardless of their location,

users can search for assets online or in archives. Everything that

WebNative displays to users comes from the heart of the FullPress server. As

soon as a file is put on the server, it is available for use. If a file is modified, the

changes are automatically made apparent through WebNative and WebNative Venture.

Unlike some systems that sit on the outside looking in, Xinet's digital asset

management solution operates right in the middle of the workflow. Because Xinet

software is based around the filesystem, it is completely and automatically

integrated into production. There is no one else optimizing workflows

and managing assets like Xinet: no one else works

so closely with the filesystem.

"Now our server produces twice as much due to FullPress' efficiency and increased business from customers. The workflow is definitely faster because we don't have to double-check our work like we did before."

CLAUS KOLB
Chief Executive Officer
Kolb Digital GmbH
(digital and commercial printer)
Munich, Germany

1 0

[Some brief considerations on the history of the poster]

É rica e densa de acontecimentos a já longa história do cartaz, produto considerado, ao menos ao longo do século XX, como elemento fundamental de comunicação, sobretudo ligado ao desenvolvimento e progresso das cidades e, mais em geral, da vida urbana. É, a este respeito, muito significativo que, desde muito cedo, apareçam referências à presença de cartazes como elementos decisivos de comunicação. Refira-se, a título de mero mas muito esclarecedor exemplo, que já o Daniel Defoe, no seu célebre Diário da Peste de Londres, descrevia há mais de duzentos anos a sua cidade, testemunhando que esta se encontrava coberta de cartazes. Sem precisar de retroceder até à época fundadora de Gutenberg ou sem procurar estudar, nos seus aspectos semiológicos ou comunicacionais, as muitas formas que o cartaz foi tomando até se volver nesta linguagem quase específica que se tornou nossa contemporânea, é preciso lembrar, ao menos, a sua época dourada, em que muitos foram os artistas que enveredaram pela sua execução, assumindo-o como veículo ideal de

The history of the poster is long, rich and eventful. It is a product considered, throughout the twentieth century at least, a fundamental component of the modern means of communication, especially in its field, with the growth and development of cities and, in more general terms, the urban way of life. In this respect it is highly significant that references to the presence of posters as decisive factors in methods of communication appear from a very early date. For a small but very revealing example of this, take a look at Daniel Defoe's famous Journal of the Plague Year, where he was already describing London as being covered

1.º CONGRESSO INTERNACIONAL DE ESTUDOS PESSOANOS / 78 Centro de Estudos Pessoanos

2

---

1 The serif font of the body text and the sans serif used in the heading are well balanced to combine text legibility with a sophisticated look. The traditional serif font is very clear, set as it is horizontally with generous leading and short lines. The display heading utilises a circular font that complements the circular setting. The reflection of the title word in the lower arc adds an interesting style feature. The visual effect is of paramount importance, so good editing is essential to avoid bad line breaks or wide spacing of words, either of which would destroy the circular effect.

2 Here is an interesting combination – one block of text is set in a wide measure, the other is a more conventional width. Wide settings can only be used successfully if the amount of text is limited, as in this case, otherwise the text becomes difficult to read..

You can change two main aspects of typefaces to give a fresh visual stimulus to your layouts: weight and style. Most types have related bold fonts, so it is easy to change the weight. The other adjustments that affect the visual look of the setting are leading and kerning.

Display
Weights, styles, leading and kerning

Consider this:

The best way of changing weight is to use a sans serif typeface. Nearly all sans serifs have versions of light, medium, bold and extra bold. Serif typefaces also have related bold fonts, but in many cases they are thickened adaptations of the original design and suffer aesthetically.

When changing styles, avoid mixing types in the same typeface classification, for example, Bembo with Garamond.

The amount of leading (the space between the lines) you use depends on the measure and the x-height and weight of the typeface. Display settings need to be varied so that the lines fit together with equal visual spacing. This setting will depend on how the ascenders and descenders fit when the lines are together.

Kerning means adjusting the amount of space between letters. Certain letters create awkward spacing when paired with one another.

Design decisions 1 Changing the weight of a typeface gives you many options. Here is Helvetica in light, medium and bold. **2** Contrasting styles – for example, text in a serif face and the heading in sans serif – works well. **3** Mixing the same category of type (that is, using two serif faces or two sans serifs) tends to clash. Here are two sans serifs from different periods, Futura and Helvetica. **4** In display, the amount of leading you select depends on how the letters fit with each other. **5** Negative leading, where the line feed is less than the point size of the type, creates visually interesting lines but may be at the expense of legibility. **6–7** In text setting, the x-height affects the amount of leading. Most sans serif faces have large x-heights and need more leading than types with small x-heights. **8** The tracking function adjusts the amount of space to the right-hand side of characters in a highlighted range. **9–10** The kerning function adjusts the amount of space between two characters. Letters with long diagonal strokes, such as A, V, W, and Y, contain more space in their zones than other letters. Compensate by changing kerning. **11** A ligature is a typographical convention in which certain characters are combined into one character. Most fonts contain ligatures for the character 'f' followed by 'i' and 'f' followed by 'l' as these are likely to merge when placed together.

Changing weight gives options

Changing weight gives options

Changing weight gives options

1

Ranged-left arrangements

If you want consistent, uniform word spacing, then a ranged-left setting style is necessary. However, if the measure is too short and the type size too big, there will be unsightly space at the end of many of the lines. Between paragraphs in this style of setting you could insert a half-line or full-line space; alternatively, you could indent the first line of each paragraph by 1 cm. You should also think about the amount of leading: remember that the readability of all typefaces is improved with leading and as a matter of course you should not use the auto setting on the computer. Always specify a specific point size for the leading.

2

Helvetica

This is Futura. Don't mix the two.

3

Sans serifs like Franklin Gothic have large x-heights and need generous leading.

6

Kerning is a useful tool for controlling the space between c h a r a c t e r s.

9

The best designers use their eyes and trust their judgement.

4

Serifs like Bembo have small x-heights so there is no real need for generous leading.

7

AV   VA
WY   YW
AW   WA
AY   YA
VW   YV

10

The best designers use their eyes and trust their judgement.

5

Tracking at -10

Tracking at 10

Tracking at 30

T r a c k i n g   a t   5 0

8

fi   fl

fi   fl

11

Exercise 17

- Select an A4 format, either portrait or landscape.
- Set 'You do not have to shout to be heard' in sans serif upper and lower case.
- Choose a size that suits the area, with sensible line breaks and no word breaks.
- Change the weights to reflect your interpretation of the copy.
- Now use negative leading, so that the letters almost touch. Finally, overlap the letters.
- Set the words 'The Language and Culture of Cartography in the Renaissance' in two lines in a size that fills the format. Set the lines solid (that is, without leading).
- Add leading and change the kerning until you achieve a good balance of space.

You do not
have to shout
to be heard

You do not
have to **shout**
to be heard

You do
not have
to shout to
be heard

Exercise 18

- Choose a serif typeface and set in capitals the words 'VARIOUS WAYS OF DRAWING WAVES'. Look at the spaces between the words and the letters.
- Make kerning changes to balance letters with too much or too little spacing. A, V and W are often problem characters.
- Now track the copy so that the words fit well within the working space.
- Compare both kerned and tracked examples with the original copy.
- Set in capitals two lines of your own text. Make sure problem characters, such as A, V and W, are shown together.
- Alter the tracking and kerning until visual equality is achieved.

VARIOUS WAYS OF
DRAWING WAVES

Original copy

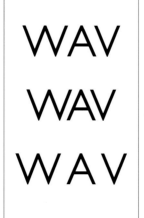

1 Original copy
2 With kerning
3 With kerning and tracking

Weights, styles, leading and kerning

*The Language and
Culture of Cartography
in the Renaissance*

*The Language and
Culture of Cartography
in the Renaissance*

VARIOUS WAYS OF
DRAWING WAVES

Copy with kerning

VARIOUS WAYS OF
DRAWING WAVES

Copy with kerning and tracking

August 27 through September 21, 2001
UNI Gallery of Art
Kamerick Art Building
University of Northern Iowa
Artist's Lecture 6 PM, Monday, August 27
101 Kamerick Art Building.
Reception to follow.

JOYCE J.

SCOTT

JOURNEYS

1

October 30 through
November 22, 200

University of Northern Iowa   Department of Art   Faculty Exhibition

PENING RECEPTION

Kamerick Art Building
Monday, October 30

7:00 PM

2

1 Panels are used in the top left-hand corner to good
effect. The large display type creates an openness that
contrasts well with the narrow panels.

2 This contemporary design was attained by clever use
of display settings. Notice the negative leading so the
figures touch the letters and the way the copy bleeds
off to the top and to each side. Legibility is maintained
while the visual interest is increased.

There are two basic setting styles that can be used in layout. One is known as symmetry, which is where the setting is based on a centred axis; this style is often referred to as 'traditional'. The other is asymmetry, where the axis is off-centred; this is seen as more dynamic and is said to create more tension.

Display
Setting styles, shapes, formats and positive to negative

Setting the page

The setting style can also reflect the shape of an accompanying picture. It is relatively easy to set the type to irregular shapes, centre it, or range it from the right.

The format of the page also influences how you set the type: landscape formats can accommodate wider measures of text, while portrait formats need shorter measures.

Changing from the positive to the negative – or 'reversing out', as it is known – adds impact to a design and gives drama to a page. To retain legibility, it is better to use a sans serif letterform when reversing out as fine serifs can be lost in the printing process.

Design decisions 1–3 Make sure you choose a measure that suits the page format. Go for short measures on portrait format and longer measures on landscape format. Centred (symmetrical) arrangements have a quiet, traditional feel, while off-centred (asymmetrical) ones create tension and look modern. **4** Symmetrical arrangements can accommodate justified settings as well as having each line centred. **5** Asymmetrical compositions can range the copy left or right. **6** Try to avoid mixing the two styles. **7** It is better to use a sans serif face when you are reversing out as the finishing strokes of a serif tend to get lost. **8** Hairline serifs should be avoided in reverse out situations as they tend to fill in unless the quality of production is very high. **9** Do not reverse out type that is smaller than 8pt.

Landscape formats allow wider measures to be used.

Short measures get lost on a landscape format.

1

Short measures look better on a portrait format.

2

Do not use long measures on a portrait format.

3

Symmetry

Justified type aligns on both the left and the right. However, this style can look visually poor if the measure is too short, as the space between words can be excessive.

Symmetry

An interesting variation is to centre each line of type on the type measure. When used in conjunction with a centred heading, this gives a strong, symmetrical appearance.

4

use a

sans

if

you can

7

Range left

Ranged-left settings with an off-centred composition give an asymmetrical arrangement. This style tends to be more dynamic than a symmetrical style of setting.

Range right

As a variation, type can be aligned on the right of the measure. This has limited use because we are used to reading type from left to right; if too many lines are set in this style, the result can be hard to read.

5

hairlines
are
dangerous

8

Stick to your style

You should never mix styles in any element of design. This looks untidy, confused and disjointed, and is difficult to follow.

Style

Make your decision before you start work and then stick to it. You will find it far easier to achieve a stylish, clear design.

6

beware

of

being too small

9

Exercise 19

- Using an A5 format, set the copy 'Keep off the Grass' in a bold sans serif face in either capitals or upper and lower case.
- Place the setting in what you consider to be the best composition.
- Repeat the exercise using Bodoni type.
- Comment on which one is the most effective.
- Now select a small piece of text of 50–60 words.
- Set this copy in 10pt type three times in three different typefaces – Bodoni, Century Schoolbook and Bembo.
- Reverse each one out of black.
- Print out and comment on the typeface legibility.
- Repeat the exercise, using a sans serif face in light, medium and bold weights.
- Set the same text in interesting shapes and with an image to see how it affects the legibility and the look of the design.

Keep off the Grass

Keep off the Grass

How it all started

The basic structure of the typefaces we use today was established by calligraphers at the end of the 15th century. They took their inspiration on the one hand from Roman capitals and on the other from the manuscript styles known as Carolingian minuscules, which were established in the reign of the Emperor Charlemagne in the latter part of the 8th century.

Exercise 20

- Select an A5 format, either landscape or portrait, and set the following copy in a serif typeface: 'Symmetry: The traditional typographic method of layout whereby lines of type are centred on the central axis of the page. Balance is achieved by equal forces.'
- Lay out in a symmetrical style.
- Set the following copy in a sans serif typeface: 'Asymmetry: The dynamic method of layout used by modernists whereby lines of type are arranged on a non-central axis. Balance is achieved by opposing forces.'
- Lay out in an asymmetrical style.
- Compare the two and observe the differences between them.

Symmetry

The traditional typographic method of layout whereby lines of type are centred on the central axis of the page. Balance is achieved by equal forces.

Asymmetry

The dynamic method of layout used by modernists whereby lines of type are arranged on a non-central axis. Balance is achieved by opposing forces.

Setting styles, shapes, formats and positive to negative

How it all started

The basic structure of the typefaces we use today was established by calligraphers at the end of the 15th century. They took their inspiration on the one hand from Roman capitals and on the other from the manuscript styles known as Carolingian minuscules, which were established in the reign of the Emperor Charlemagne in the latter part of the 8th century.

How it all started

The basic structure of the typefaces we use today was established by calligraphers at the end of the 15th century. They took their inspiration on the one hand from Roman capitals and on the other from the manuscript styles known as Carolingian minuscules, which were established in the reign of the Emperor Charlemagne in the latter part of the 8th century.

How it all started

The basic structure of the typefaces we use today was established by calligraphers at the end of the 15th century. They took their inspiration on the one hand from Roman capitals and on the other from the manuscript styles known as Carolingian minuscules, which were established in the reign of the Emperor Charlemagne in the latter part of the 8th century.

It came from
outer space

Irregular shapes are easy to achieve with computer setting. They will add visual interest to a piece of text and at the same time they can reflect the contents.

It came from
outer space

Irregular shapes are easy to achieve with computer setting. They will add visual interest to a piece of text and at the same time they can reflect the contents.

It came from
OUTER SPACE

Irregular shapes are easy to achieve with computer setting. They will add visual interest to a piece of text and can reflect the contents.

Rules (printed lines) and ornaments serve a functional role by directing the reader's eye around the page or drawing attention to specific parts of the copy. They can also be used as decorative features, or embellishments.

Display
Rules and ornaments

These can be used in both text and display settings

Rules are available in a range of thicknesses and styles (continuous lines, dotted lines, dashes, for example). The widths range from a half point (hairline) upwards. When used in conjunction with text settings, rules help the reader to clarify information and separate items. Used vertically, they divide columns of text. Horizontally, they are a means of organising information and helping readability. They can be used to underline words and emphasise text.

In display setting, rules can create drama and act as attention seekers. If they are wide enough, type can be reversed out of them. In poster work, rules can also act as an information identifier.

Ornaments – also known as flowers – have always been used by printers and designers to embellish a page. This emanates from medieval books which were widely ornamented, their pages decorated with painted borders. The most popular method of decorating text with ornaments is to insert Zapf Dingbats or any equivalents.

Design decisions 1 In tabular matter, rules are used to organise information into categories. **2** They help to guide the eye across the items. **3** Rules are very helpful in contents pages. **4** In display settings, rules can be used to underscore the type as a contrast to the height of type. For example, a heading set in 36pt Univers light with very heavy rules as an underscore. Conversely a very black, heavy type could be underscored with a light rule. **5** Rules can be used to direct attention to a piece of copy to be highlighted within the text. **6** Ornaments give a traditional feel.

Title	Name	
Address		
		Postcode
Email		
Tel	Fax	

1

Series D				
The Fairy Queen	10	September	20.30h	2
Ariadne auf Naxos	23	October	20.30h	19
Recital Gosta Winbergh	7	January	20.30h	53
Norma	14	January	20.30h	59
Pikovia Dama	7	February	20.30h	67
Il viaggio a Reims	12	March	20.30h	78
Orfeo ed Euridice	16	April	20.30h	96

2

Contents

3

In magazine work, typographers must constantly look for ways of attracting attention and stimulating the reader.

Rules draw attention to subheads

The way subheadings and headings are positioned is one method of bringing the reader into the text. Rules can give dramatic tension to a heading.

5

Univers
Light

4

Univers
Black

BRITISH PAINTING

1948–1964

6

Exercise 21

- Using an A5 format, set the contents page of any book. The type size, measure and leading are at your discretion. The page numbers should align right.
- Using the same setting, place hairline or 1pt rules below each item.
- Comment on the two versions.

Contents

Introduction	6
Basic Design Principles	8
Basic Shapes	14
Balance and Harmony	26
Design Projects and Categories	86
Magazine	102
Index	128

Contents

Introduction	6
Basic Design Principles	8
Basic Shapes	14
Balance and Harmony	26
Design Projects and Categories	86
Magazine	102
Index	128

Exercise 22

- Using the same format as in exercise 21, set the line 'Rules have Power' three times in either capital letters or a combination of upper and lower case.
- Set the first example in a 36pt light sans serif face. Underscore the text with 12pt rules.
- Then set the text in a 36pt medium sans serif face. Underscore it with 6pt rules.
- Set the text in a 36pt bold or extra bold sans·serif face. Underscore it with 1pt rules.
- Analyse the different versions.

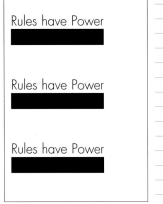

Rules have Power

Rules have Power

Rules have Power

Rules have Power

Rules have Power

Rules have Power

Rules have Power

Rules have Power

Rules have Power

We *make our* CUSTOMERS *and keep their* COMPUTERS *(and* | productive | safe | reliable. | Anywhere. | Anytime.

Getting more

from·what you've

already got.

AT SYMANTEC, WE'RE DEDICATED to the notion that computing should be simpler, faster, and more productive.

That's why we build products that automatically resolve problems, or make things easier to do.

Take our *Norton Utilities™* software, for example. If the information on your PC is mission critical—and what business information isn't?—*Norton Utilities* gives you peace of mind by protecting the integrity of your data and keeps your system running at peak performance. With *Norton Utilities*, you can always count on the comfort of knowing that if it isn't broken, we'll fix it anyway.

Our *Norton AntiVirus™* products operate under the same preventive-medicine principle: it is better to not have a virus than to recover from one. Which is why we've set up the Symantec AntiVirus Research Centers (SARC™)— world-renowned research institutes devoted to locating viruses and rooting them out. So you can get on with your work without having to worry.

How can a contact manager make you more productive? By doing a lot more than just holding names and addresses. Our *ACT!™* software gives you all the information you need to stay on top of managing every aspect of all your business relationships. And if you're working away from the home office, products such as *pcANYWHERE™* and *WinFax PRO™* will make things so familiar as to make you think you're right at your own desk.

What about the Internet? With technologies changing so rapidly, your developers need a set of tools that will allow them to get their web development applications to market before they become obsolete. This is precisely the idea behind our award-winning *Symantec Café™* series of authoring products. With *Symantec Café*, it's extremely easy for both novice and experienced programmers alike to develop dynamic Java™ applications and applets.

And because business these days is more global than ever, it's important that people anywhere feel comfortable with our products. So we adapt our software to local markets and cultures—18 languages and counting.

Add it all up and you'll find that you have a multitude of ways to make life on your PC easier, better, and more rewarding.

Who could ask for more?

1

viewpoint

Gas Reform in Ukraine

Monopolies Markets Corruption

Private Participation in theReform of the natural gas industry in Ukraine started a year later than reform of the power industry. Because gas reform had no blueprint, its direction has remained ambiguous. Private Participation in theReform of the natural gas industry in Ukraine started a year later than reform of the power industry. Because gas reform had no blueprint, its direction has remained ambiguous. PrivatParticipation in theReform of the natural gas industry in Ukraine started a year later than reform of the power industry. Because gas reform had no blueprint, its direction has remained ambiguous.

Reform of the natural gas industry in Ukraine started a year later than reform of the power industry. Because gas reform had no blueprint, its direction has remained ambiguous. Reform of the natural gas industry in Ukraine started a year later than reform of the power industry. Because gas reform had no blueprint, its direction has remained ambiguous. Reform of the natural gas industry in Ukraine started a year later than reform of the power industry. Because gas reform had no blueprint, its direction has remained ambiguous. Reform of the natural gas industry in Ukraine started a year later than reform of the power industry. Because gas reform had no blueprint, its has remained ambiguous.

Private Participation in theReform of the natural gas industry in Ukraine started a year later than reform of the power industry. Because gas reform had no blueprint, its direction has remained ambiguous. Private Participation in theReform of the natural gas industry in Ukraine started a year later than reform of the power industry. Because gas reform had no blueprint, its direction has remained ambiguous. PrivatParticipation in theReform of the natural gas industry in Ukraine started a year later than reform of the power industry. Because gas reform had no blueprint, its direction has remained

natural gas industry in Ukraine started a year later than reform of the power industry. Because gas reform had no blueprint, its direction has remained ambiguous. Private Participation in theReform of the natural gas industry in Ukraine started a year later than reform of the power industry. Because gas reform had no blueprint, its direction has remained ambiguous. PrivatParticipation in theReform of the natural gas industry in Ukraine started a year later than reform of the power industry. Because gas reform had no blueprint, its direction has remained ambiguous.

2

1 Here is an example of how rules can be used with both small and large type. In the heading and the header they add emphasis to the copy and provide a style feature and decoration. The heading is particularly interesting where the rules run through the letter descenders.

2 Rules above and below the title focus attention on this; type within the lower rule contributes an additional functional appeal. Vertical rules delineate the running text, giving the grid a clear structure and achieving maximum readability.

Colour is the most exciting visual element that a designer deals with. It adds variety and mood to a design and also adds a spatial dimension. Designers today are fortunate: software programs make it much easier to use and manipulate colour than it was in the past.

Colour Message

Selecting colours

Just as a typeface 'speaks' to us, so too does colour. It is important to remember that colours have symbolic associations. Red, for example, is associated with fire and is thought of as warm and energetic, while blue is tranquil and cool. The colours you choose have a tremendous impact on the moods of your designs and the way people respond to them.

Particular combinations of colours also create moods. To create a feeling of harmony, use analagous colours – ones that are close to each other on the colour wheel, such as blues and greens. For more tension and vibrancy, use contrasting colours that are opposite each other on the colour wheel, such as red and green. This combination tends to clash, but will quickly attract and generate excitement.

Design decisions 1–2 Some colours appear to advance, while others seem to recede. If you want to make something seem to come towards the viewer, warm colours such as reds and oranges are the best ones to choose. **3–4** Blues and greens seem to recede when set next to a red. **5** Harmonious colours are close to each other on the colour wheel, such as yellow and green, or blue and green. Complementary colours are ones that are opposite each other on the colour wheel – red and green, or yellow and violet. These combinations are vibrant and full of tension. **6** Yellows are softer and less strident than reds. **7** There are many different colour strengths within each hue (see page 58); by changing the type (or tone), you can create many variations within the same hue.

advance   **advance**

1

2

3

4

recede   **recede**

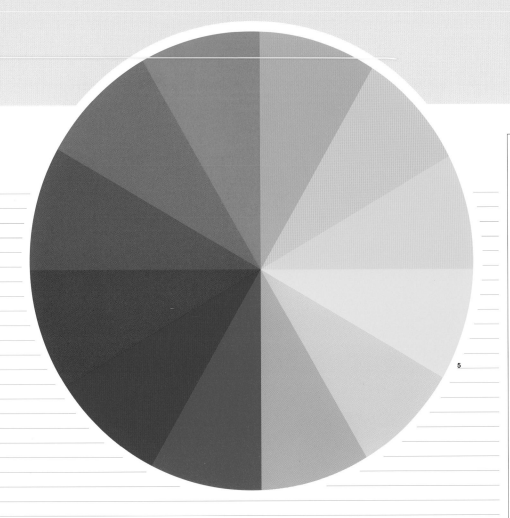

5

There are many intensities

rock'n'roll

rock'n'roll

rock'n'roll

rock'n'roll

rock'n'roll

Do these colours advance or recede?

7

I'm red and aggressive

I'm softer in yellow

6

Exercise 23

- Using an A6 format, set the word 'BRAVO!' in capitals in a bold sans serif typeface. Print it in a bright red.
- Repeat this exercise using cyan.
- Put the two print-outs side by side and compare them.
- Using the same format, typeface and type size, set the words 'JAZZ BAR'. Again, print it in red and blue, but this time try to get the colours to recede by using different strengths.

BRAVO!

BRAVO!

JAZZ BAR

JAZZ BAR

Exercise 24

- Using the same format, type style and colours as in exercise 23, change the backgrounds to red on black and red on yellow.
- Repeat this exercise, using words and colours of your own choice to see how different backgrounds complement and affect different messages.
- Print out and compare them.

BRAVO!

BRAVO!

JAZZ BAR

JAZZ BAR

1 Colour can differentiate items in both display
and text. Here it has been used very
effectively to show two languages. Reversing
out of a solid colour is relatively easy to do
and gives an added dimension to a design.

2 This example illustrates an extremely good
use of colour. The word 'inside' recedes into
the background giving a perfect reflection of
the meaning of the copy.

3 The two primary colours selected show how
the concept of a design can be reinforced
by colour. In addition to this it also defines
the copy.

With the tremendous explosion of possibilities that colour brings, comes a need for discipline: do not overuse colour, or its impact will be lost.

Colour
Differences and legibility

Colour terminology

There are three terms that you need to understand when working with colour: hue – the pure colour (as in red, blue and green); tone – the relative lightness or darkness of a colour; and saturation – a scale from fully intense as in a bright red to low intensity as in a dark green.

When using type and colour, legibility comes from contrast. The greatest contrast is between black type on a white background; the least contrast is yellow type on a white background. The range between these two is extensive. As the background moves closer to the type in colour, so legibility decreases.

Design decisions 1 Colour is described in three ways. **2** Hue, the name of a colour **3** Tone, a range from light to dark **4** Saturation, a range from low intensity to full intensity. **5–6** The strongest contrasts are black type on a white background or yellow type on a black background. **7** The weakest contrast is yellow type on a white background. **8–10** As type and background colours move closer together, legibility decreases. **11** The design of the type also affects the way the colour appears. A serif typeface does not have a big surface to carry the colour, weakening its intensity and making it appear lighter than the original colour chosen. **12–13** A sans or slab serif typeface can carry the colour better, maintaining its intensity.

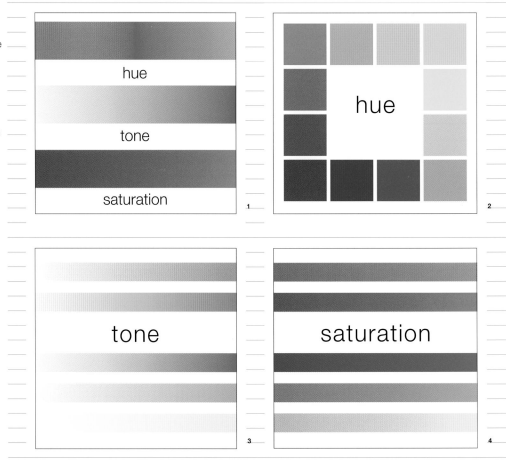

Taxi

Taxi

Taxi

Taxi

Taxi

Taxi

Taxi

Taxi

Taxi

5

6

7

8

9

10

11

12

13

Exercise 25

- Select an A4 landscape format.
- Set the word 'OK!' in a bold sans serif typeface. Print it in yellow on a white background.
- Repeat the exercise, moving through the colours of the spectrum – orange, red, green, blue and violet.
- Analyse your results and ascertain which colours advance and which ones recede.
- Experiment with the background and text colours to achieve minimum and maximum contrast.

Exercise 26

- Using the same format as in exercise 25, set the words 'Bar Manager' in 12pt Bembo. Print it in red on a white background.
- Repeat the exercise, changing the type to a 12pt bold sans serif typeface.
- Look at the two print-outs and decide which typeface appears to have the most intense colour.

Differences and legibility

1 The colours are harmonious because of their
intensity; however, they give a bold
impression that suits this image.

2 A good example of using colour to advance
and recede the image. By simply changing
the background colour the whole visual feel
of this design is altered and a diffferent
perspective realised.

3 The use of tints of a colour can soften the
image and lighten the mood. Here the tint of
orange gives a spacious feel to the design.

4 Two very intense colours have created an
aggressive mood.

1

2

3

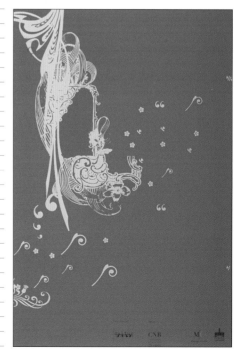

4

With the range of sophisticated software and printers available today, mixing type, colour and pictures is quick and easy – and produces fantastic results.

Colour
Mixing type, colour and pictures

Colour impact

Five- and six-colour machines are available in production so a designer can utilise the four-colour process (CMYK) and one or two pantone colours to achieve maximum colour effect.

CMYK is known as the subtractive colour system and utilises the colours cyan, magenta, yellow and key (black). This system is used primarily by printers. The four CMYK colours are combined to produce other colours.

Pantone colours are premixed to achieve a single unique colour. These are standardised so that the printer and designer can access the same pantone colour by reference to its number.

These systems enable designers to use the full range of colours and colour tints to recreate the original colour of artworks and photographs.

Colour can be used as the background to show off the type or blend it into the page. A good example of this is to create a box and fill it with a light tone of a less intense colour – say a 20 per cent yellow – which acts as a good background on which to place black text. Gradations of colour can be used imaginatively to give visual excitement to a background. Similarly different colours and different gradations of the same colour can be used to change text emphasis. For the sake of legibility, only use colour tints on larger display type.

1

Design decisions 1 In large display type, colour can create interesting new shapes when the letterforms overlap. **2** When two colours overlap, a third colour is formed, giving added visual interest. **3** There is a great contrast between the white of the text and the deep blue of the sky, making the caption very easy to read. This reverse-out style is also an economic use of the empty space on the photograph. **4** Backgrounds can be subtly coloured, producing good surfaces on which to place text. **5** Introducing coloured box rules is another way of adding visual variety. **6–8** Gradations of colour also add visual interest.

2

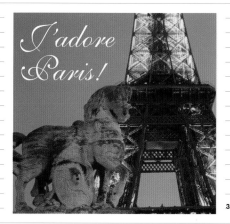

J'adore Paris!

3

The creativity of colour

Colour attracts the reader: it opens up the whole design and gives an added dimension to the visual look of a piece. By changing the density of the colour you are using, you can make it look as if another colour is being used — and, of course, it creates contrast within the overall composition.

4

The creativity of colour

Colour attracts the reader: it opens up the whole design and gives an added dimension to the visual look of a piece. By changing the density of the colour you are using, you can make it look as if another colour is being used — and, of course, it creates contrast within the overall composition.

5

The creativity of colour

Colour attracts the reader: it opens up the whole design and gives an added dimension to the visual look of a piece. By changing the density of the colour you are using, you can make it look as if another colour is being used — and, of course, it creates contrast within the overall composition.

6

The creativity of colour

Colour attracts the reader: it opens up the whole design and gives an added dimension to the visual look of a piece. By changing the density of the colour you are using, you can make it look as if another colour is being used — and, of course, it creates contrast within the overall composition.

7

The creativity of colour

Colour attracts the reader: it opens up the whole design and gives an added dimension to the visual look of a piece. By changing the density of the colour you are using, you can make it look as if another colour is being used — and, of course, it creates contrast within the overall composition.

8

Exercise 27

- Select an A5 landscape format.
- Set several numbers in a type size big enough to fill the central area of the space.
- Choose two primary colours.
- Overlap the numbers in different colours, creating new shapes where the overlapping occurs.
- The secondary colour forms where the two primary colours meet.

Exercise 28

- Using the same format as in exercise 27, create a box 7.5cm (3 in) square. Fill it with a 20 per cent yellow.
- Set 30 words of copy in a 10pt sans serif typeface.
- Print this text in black on the 20 per cent yellow background.
- Repeat the exercise, placing a 2pt rule around the edge of the box, and print in 60 per cent of the yellow.
- Experiment by increasing the background to its full tonal value.
- Comment on your experiment.
- Using the same size box, graduate the background from top to bottom in a single colour.
- Experiment with the colour of the background, type and the colour and direction of the blend.

One of the big advantages of using a computer is the speed with which you can change the look of the design. It is easy to experiment with background and text colours.

One of the big advantages of using a computer is the speed with which you can change the look of the design. It is easy to experiment with background and text colours.

One of the big advantages of using a computer is the speed with which you can change the look of the design. It is easy to experiment with background and text colours.

One of the big advantages of using a computer is the speed with which you can change the look of the design. It is easy to experiment with background and text colours.

1 In this attractive example, the colour helps define separate items of copy. It also gives added visual meaning to the image and copy.

2 Colour is a good way of emphasising items. The use of a bright colour for image and text demonstrates this.

3 The grey acts as a neutral colour harmonising text and image. Using neutral colours can reduce conflict that may arise if colours are loud or intense.

4 A lovely use of a soft colour to contrast but harmonise with the darker figures in the picture.

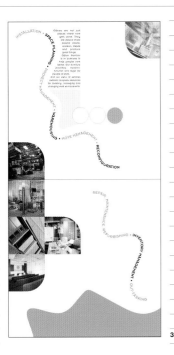

Before you make any decisions on type selection, you need to decide on the priorities within the text. This means establishing hierarchies (an order of emphasis), so that you know how many different levels of information you're dealing with.

Analysing information
Hierarchies of text

Levels of importance

With headings you might have three levels of importance, which you could term A, B and C. The text also needs to be classified in some way, so that you can establish a standard style of setting for each level of information.

Different levels of display heading can be created by changing the size or weight. With text settings, size is one way of differentiating things. In addition, a change of typestyle (for example, from sans serif to serif) always creates visual interest. Lastly, you can use colour.

Design decisions 1 This music programme has five levels of importance: programme number, date, time, composer, and piece of music and performers. **2** In display hierarchies, contrasts in form (for example, changing from roman to italic) and colour are a good way of achieving clarity. **3** Or a contrast in type style. **4** When display and text settings are brought together, different sizes and styles can easily be used. **5** Rules can also play a part in the hierarchy. **6** Boxes can be used to emphasise text.

37 Saturday August 17
7.30pm–9.50pm

Rodgers, orch. Hans Spialek Babes in Arms – Overture **Rodgers, orch. Robert Russell Bennett** Victory at Sea – Symphonic Scenario; On Your Toes – Slaughter on Tenth Avenue **Rodgers & Hammerstein** Oklahoma! (concert version)
Maureen Lipman, Lisa Vroman
Klea Blackhurst, Tim Flavin, Brent Barrett

1

Wednesday
● **Susan Bullock**
Soprano joins the South Quarter Sinfonia for works by Ravel and Wagner.
St Mark's Chapel (07 22 1061)
7.30pm £8–£15.
● **Ian Fountain**
Piano works by Beethoven.
St James's church
(02 38 0441)
7.30pm £7–£13.

2

36
FAMILY FAVOURITES
Cornish Ware brought to book.

38
LATE QUARTET
Linen Works: a group of weavers with more than one string to their bow.

42
TIME FOR CRAFTS TO GO TO THE BALL
Arts for Everyone – will the new lottery scheme live up to its name?

44
SOURCES OF INSPIRATION
The sculptor Bryan Illsley talks about his life and work.

3

House Specialties

SERVED WITH PILAU RICE

Chicken Passanda.........£6.50

A mild and delightful dish, specially cut slices of chicken marinated with yoghurt based sauce and cooked in fresh cream, mixed ground nuts and almond powder.

Karhai Lamb...............£6.50

Tender pieces of lamb grilled in a tandoori oven, cooked with garlic, ginger, tomatoes, onions, capsicum and fresh coriander, medium spiced.

Karhai King Prawn.......£8.95

Achar Gost.................£6.50

A fairly hot dish. Pieces of marinated lamb cooked in a tantalizing pickle masala, laced with whole green chillies.

Amere Murgh..............£6.50

A delightful mild chicken dish, cooked with pulp mango, mild spices, fresh cream and almonds.

4

Best Saving Rates

Find the best deals on savings accounts

PROVIDER	PRODUCT	GROSS RATE
£1/£10 to invest		
Rock	Online Saver	3.35
Net	Online Saver	3.05
Local Friendly	Immediate Access	3.00
£1,000 to invest		
Southern Reliant	Saver Plus	3.40
Roots	Online Saver	3.35
BankDirect	Saver Plus	3.22
£25,000 to invest		
BankDirect	Midi Longterm	3.40
Roots	Saver Plus	3.35
Local Friendly	Midi	3.25
£50,000 to invest		
Roots	30 Day Access	4.20
Net	3 Year Access	3.75
Local Friendly	2 Year Access	3.55
Southern Reliant	Midi Mini	3.45
Lane and Lane	Midi Saver	3.40
Over £50,000 to invest		
Lane and Lane	Midi Maxi Longterm	5.55
Northern Circle	Fixed Saversure	5.20
Southern Reliant	Fixed Saversure	4.75
Local Friendly	Saversure Access (variable)	4.70
Net	Premier Plus	4.65

5

DVD & VIDEO

The Magnificent Seven
Stylish

★★★☆☆

Starring: Steve McQueen, James Coburn, Charles Bronson, Robert Vaughn and Yul Brynner. The beleaguered denizens of a Mexican village, weary of attacks by banditos, hire seven gunslingers to repel the invaders. This is without a doubt a film to remember.

Gone with the Wind
Old classic – not to be missed

★★★☆☆

More than a movie: this 1939 epic (and all-time box-office champ) is superbly emotional and nostalgic. Vivien Leigh is magnificent; Clark Gable provides one of the most charismatic performances ever. It's an achievement that pushed its every resource – art direction, colour, sound, cinematography – to new limits.

A Beautiful Mind
High interest

★★★★★

A decent biopic of the Nobel prize-winning mathematician, John Nash. It doesn't come close to conveying the contribution Nash made to economics, and it's really just Shine with sums, repeating as it does one of Hollywood's favourite equations – genius equals madness.

6

Exercise 29

- Using an A5 portrait page, set an article 200 words long in 9 or 11pt text.
- Analyse the copy and write some main headings, subheadings, and any other features you feel are relevant.
- Using the same format, set in eight levels of hierarchy, using a variety of sizes, forms, and weights, the following:
1/Friday July 19/7:30pm/Haydn/The Creation/featuring/Christiane Delze/Soprano
- Experiment with the type, colour, and style.

Each year the second year students, in conjunction with their Contextual Studies program, produce a course magazine. The subject matter relates to the design industry. Each student is required to write approximately 500–750 words on a subject of choice, research the appropriate visual material, and bring these elements together in a design for a double-page spread.

The objective of this project is to enable students to oversee a complete concept from the selection of the subject matter and writing of an article, to the design and production of the magazine.

Students are encouraged to: use their writing skills; analyse subject matter; make constructive critical comments.

The subject matter for the article is of the student's own choosing, thus motivating them to choose a subject of interest. This in turn encourages care and clarity in the treatment of the text and the use of language.

The work is assessed according to the following guidelines: the student's ability to evaluate in written form a design topic; the application of appropriate visual material to improve the article and provide an effective design; ability to meet production deadlines.

Magazine Design Project

Each year the second year students, in conjunction with their Contextual Studies program, produce a course magazine. The subject matter relates to the design industry. Each student is required to write approximately 500–750 words on a subject of choice, research the appropriate visual material, and bring these elements together in a design for a double-page spread.

Aims and Objectives:
The objective of this project is to enable students to oversee a complete concept from the selection of the subject matter and writing of an article, to the design and production of the magazine.
Students are encouraged to:
- use their writing skills
- analyse subject matter
- make constructive critical comments.
The subject matter for the article is of the student's own choosing, thus motivating them to choose a subject of interest. This in turn encourages care and clarity in the treatment of the text and the use of language.

Assessment criteria:
The work is assessed according to the following guidelines:
1. The student's ability to evaluate in written form a design topic.
2. The application of appropriate visual material to improve the article and provide an effective design.
3. Ability to meet production deadlines.

Exercise 30

- Select an article 200 words long. Set it as straight text in 10pt Times on an A5 page.
- Analyse the copy and insert a main heading and subheadings that show the order of priority.
- Set up a two-column grid on an A4-square page. Flow in text and headings, and style.
- Set up a two-column grid on the same size page. Flow in the text with the headings. Now introduce two photographs, and style.

Graffiti is a contentious subject. It can be viewed either as vandalism or as an art form. On the one hand people argue that it damages our environment and should not be condoned; on the other hand it is seen to have an intense energy and creativity. Whatever your opinion, you cannot ignore the fact that graffiti is now part of urban life. The essence of the best graffiti can be utilised as a starting point for design concepts. Speed, vigor, and excitement are inseparable from graffiti art. This is because it is usually an illicit activity. Its clandestine nature is in itself a motivating force and dictates the type of equipment used: spray cans or broad-tipped markers – easily carried, effective, and fast. The rich visual dynamism of designed mark-making conveys a great sense of enjoyment that may well be echoed in the viewer: Graffiti has many lessons to offer in color and pattern. There are uses and applications for this questionable street art. Urban locations have been designated for this very purpose. Record covers, posters, comics, and badges use this medium to capture the essence of a message and convey it in an interesting and powerful way.

Graffiti

Graffiti is a contentious subject. It can be viewed either as vandalism or as an art form. On the one hand people argue that it damages our environment and should not be condoned; on the other hand it is seen to have an intense energy and creativity.

Not to be ignored
Whatever your opinion, you cannot ignore the fact that graffiti is now part of urban life. The essence of the best graffiti can be utilised as a starting point for design concepts. Speed, vigor, and excitement are inseparable from graffiti art. This is because it is usually an illicit activity. Its clandestine nature is in itself a motivating force and dictates the type of equipment used: spray cans or broad-tipped markers – easily carried, effective, and fast.

Street art
The rich visual dynamism of designed mark-making conveys a great sense of enjoyment that may well be echoed in the viewer: Graffiti has many lessons to offer in color and pattern. There are uses and applications for this questionable street art. Urban locations have been designated for this very purpose.

Record covers, posters, comics, and badges use this medium to capture the essence of a message and convey it in an interesting and powerful way.

1

Friday July 19 7.30 pm

Haydn

The Creation

FEATURING

Christine Delze

Soprano

1

H A Y D N

The Creation

FEATURING

Christine Delze
Soprano

FRIDAY JULY 19
7.30 PM

Graffiti

Graffiti is a contentious subject. It can be viewed either as vandalism or as an art form. On the one hand people argue that it damages our environment and should not be condoned; on the other hand it is seen to have an intense energy and creativity.

Not to be ignored
Whatever your opinion, you cannot ignore the fact that graffiti is now part of urban life. The essence of the best graffiti can be utilised as a starting point for design concepts. Speed, vigor, and excitement are inseparable from graffiti art. This is because it is usually an illicit activity. Its clandestine nature is in itself a motivating force and dictates the type of equipment used: spray cans or broad-tipped markers – easily carried, effective, and fast.

Street art
The rich visual dynamism of designed mark-making conveys a great sense of enjoyment that may well be echoed in the viewer: Graffiti has many lessons to offer in color and pattern. There are uses and applications for this questionable street art. Urban locations have been designated for this very purpose.

Record covers, posters, comics, and badges use this medium to capture the essence of a message and convey it in an interesting and powerful way.

Graffiti

Graffiti is a contentious subject. It can be viewed either as vandalism or as an art form. On the one hand people argue that it damages our environment and should not be condoned; on the other hand it is seen to have an intense energy and creativity.

Not to be ignored
Whatever your opinion, you cannot ignore the fact that graffiti is now part of urban life. The essence of the best graffiti can be utilised as a starting point for design concepts. Speed, vigor, and excitement are inseparable from graffiti art. This is because it is usually an illicit activity. Its clandestine nature is in itself a motivating force and dictates the type of equipment used: spray cans or broad-tipped markers – easily carried, effective, and fast.

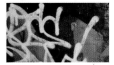

Street art
The rich visual dynamism of designed mark-making conveys a great sense of enjoyment that may well be echoed in the viewer: Graffiti has many lessons to offer in color and pattern. There are uses and applications for this questionable street art. Urban locations have been designated for this very purpose.

Record covers, posters, comics, and badges use this medium to capture the essence of a message and convey it in an interesting and powerful way.

In certain respects, an illustration or diagram can be far more dynamic and imaginative than a photograph. Illustration has the potential to dramatise the subject and to emphasise certain aspects.

Analysing information
Illustration and diagram

Illustration as informer

In information design, the point of using illustrations is to make complex issues clear and deliver information. There are many reasons for using illustrations: they can help the reader to work out instructions, show how to do things, guide people to destinations, transcend language barriers, create emotional responses and even illustrate scenarios that do not yet exist.

As a designer, you can use the computer to create maps and diagrams and generate drawings. The important thing is to know what constitutes good practice. Make sure any wording can be read and that the diagram makes things easier rather than complicating them. Remember the old adage: 'less is more'.

Design decisions 1 Maps are good examples of diagrams that are used to inform people. This one is made particularly clear through the addition of 3-dimensional elements.
2 Illustrations can be used to explain products. A camera is a complex piece of apparatus – labelling its parts on a simple diagram helps avoid confusion and lack of clarity.
3 Had this illustration been described in words, complicated, boring text could have resulted. This image is attractive, it does not use much space, and it is very easy to understand at a glance.

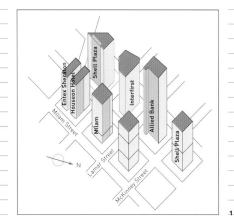

1

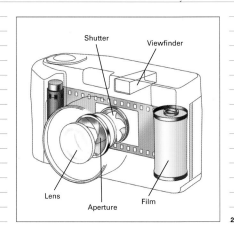

2

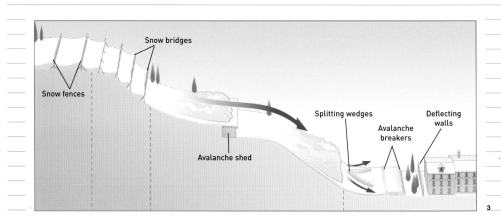

3

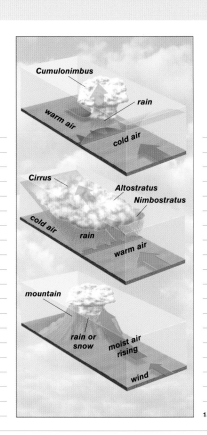

1 This clear, simple diagram conveys a lot
  of information – written as text, this
  would be heavy and complicated.
2 An excellent example of how an image is
  reinforced by use of diagram. The arrows
  and graphic symbols give emphasis to
  the point being made by the image.

Exercise 31

- Using a portrait A5 format, devise a map leading from your home to the local library, showing interesting and important landmarks and including information on public transport.
- Devise a map showing the cultural venues in your town, including any churches and historic buildings, cinemas, theatres, clubs, bars, and so on. Include a key if you think it will help.

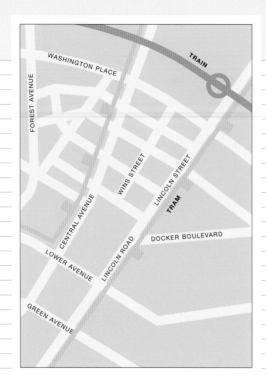

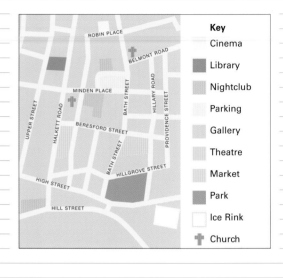

Exercise 32

- Using the same format as in exercise 31, devise a step-by-step sequence showing a simple, everyday experience such as making a cup of tea, using a book index, boiling an egg, sewing on a button or potting a plant.
- Design the sequence so that it covers between four and eight steps, each one measuring 5cm (2 in) square.
- Write short explanatory text for each box and lay it out on an A5 page with an appropriate heading.

Potting Plants

When you buy a new plant, remove approximately one-third of the growth and thin out the branches. This will give the plant a good basis for growth.

The root system will be enormous when new. In spring, reduce the root system by one-third so that the plant does not become pot-bound.

If you wish to transfer the plant into a new pot it is best to do this when root pruning. Allow the foliage to grow quite freely at this stage, this will help the plant to establish itself within the new pot.

Keep trimming the branches to encourage the plant to grow. Sunlight and occasional watering are also required to keep your plant in peak condition.

1 This is a busy design that effectively conveys information.
The changes in the size of the copy and the integration of
words and diagram make for a compelling composition.

2 Lists can be given visual impact by changing colour or
weight of type for the items of information. The map on
the right is simple and easy to follow.

3 The words 'Design is a way of looking at and improving
the world around us' are perfectly complemented by the
stylish design in this well-balanced, harmonious example.

4 It is a clever idea to have the very large display type very
much out of focus as this concentrates the eye on the
information placed inbetween.

Because we are so used to seeing photographic images of real-life events on television and in the press, photographs somehow seem more 'real' and trustworthy than illustrations. As a result, designers often tend to use photographs to get across a particular message.

Photography
Making decisions

Using photographs

You can take your own images, employ a photographer or consult one of the many photographic libraries that have thousands of images at the ready. You can also use sophisticated software programs such as Adobe Photoshop to manipulate and enhance the images.

To use photographic images effectively, you need to understand how to create dynamic compositions and, perhaps more importantly, how to integrate the photograph with the copy.

Design decisions There are various techniques that you can use with photographs. **1** Photocollage is a useful way of conveying a visual message that consists of a number of elements. **2–6** Computer programs such as Adobe Photoshop offer many ways of making an image visually more attractive; you can change the colour and screen structures, and if needs be exaggerate them. **7** A simple black-and-white image can be made livelier by using it as a duotone – here black with blue. **8** Unusual and unexpected effects add impact. **9–12** Using photographs in unusual shapes can also liven up the design.

1

2

3

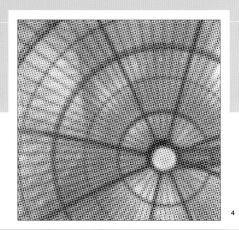

4

5

6

7

8

9

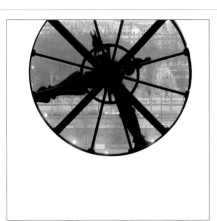

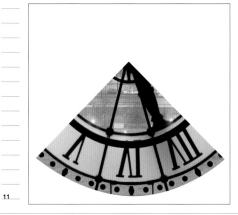

10

11

12

Exercise 33

- Using an A4 format, design a double-page spread for a magazine.
- The subject is action. Choose any sporting activity, amateur or professional, or any action involving people or animals.
- Select from as many photographs as possible.
- Decide on six to eight photographs for the project, using shots that are as varied as possible. Write captions explaining each photograph.
- Design a grid to accommodate the photographs and the captions.
- Using your images and captions, produce a dynamic spread with a good contrast in subject matter, shapes of photographs and sizes of image.

Young dancers can sweep the floor

The aim of running text around a photograph is to make the words fit with the shape of the photograph without leaving unattractive and clumsy gaps.

Right
You should not insert too much spacing between words to push them out to fit the shape; instead you could add or delete words.

Contrast is an essential element in design. Whether it be in size, color, form, shape, or composition and balance. Here the size difference works well: the cut-out halftone contrasts with the sequence of squared-up halftones.

Practice makes perfect
Running a picture across folds can be hazardous but it can work if you are careful to avoid placing it in such a way that you lose critical parts of the image.

Below left to right
Bleeding off photographs also adds visual interest, but make sure you do not bleed off important areas of the image. Add captions to photographs that are not self explanatory

Exercise 34

- Using the same format and grid as in exercise 33, change the subject to your home town or village.
- Use six to eight photographs that symbolise its attractiveness to you. The subject matter could be architecture, local people, street signs, etc.
- Introduce contrasts in subject matter, shapes and sizes.
- Write a suitable caption for each image.

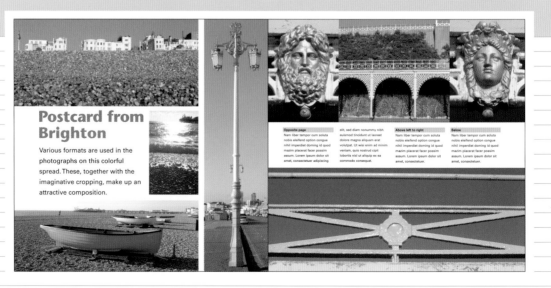

Postcard from Brighton

Various formats are used in the photographs on this colorful spread. These, together with the imaginative cropping, make up an attractive composition.

Opposite page
Nam liber tempor cum soluta nobis eleifend option congue nihil imperdiet doming id quod mazim placerat facer possim assum. Lorem ipsum dolor sit amet, consectetuer adipiscing

elit, sed diam nonummy nibh euismod tincidunt ut laoreet dolore magna aliquam erat volutpat. Ut wisi enim ad minim veniam, quis nostrud cipit lobortis nisl ut aliquip ex ea commodo consequat.

Above left to right
Nam liber tempor cum soluta nobis eleifend option congue nihil imperdiet doming id quod mazim placerat facer possim assum. Lorem ipsum dolor sit amet, consectetuer.

Below
Nam liber tempor cum soluta nobis eleifend option congue nihil imperdiet doming id quod mazim placerat facer possim assum. Lorem ipsum dolor sit amet, consectetuer.

1

A good meal is a work of theater. Ideally, it unfolds gracefully, with Act One setting the stage for things to come. In many households, appetizers may be considered a first course when guests are seated at the table. But in this chapter, we think of them as munchables: tiny morsels that can be enjoyed prior to sitting down for the main act.

These simple snacks, when placed on an artful serving dish and accompanied with a fitting aperitif, can somehow transform a room's atmosphere from mundane to sublime.

Typically, the French beer wine or wine-based drinks as aperitifs. Mixed drinks à l'américaine have caught on in the Old World, too, with gin and Scotch enjoying increasing popularity. Depending on your mood and the menu, however, consideration should be given to the fact that a lighter styled wine-based opener will prepare and stimulate the palate in a more gentle way than a spirit based one.

Any wine can serve as an aperitif, but one with a cool, refreshing quality will titillate the taste buds, simultaneously satisfying and arousing them. We shy away from tiny, full bodied reds at the beginning of a meal, for they are a trifle harsh to sip

as a starter. Sparkling wines, however, with their fresh, vivacious flavors and texture, make a particularly fine opening beverage. There is a festive air that surrounds bubbly as well; it seems to celebrate an imminent dining experience.

Because of their inconsequentially character, varietal wines such as Riesling and Gewürztraminer also make excellent introductory statements. They pair well with both finger foods and first courses. Chardonnay and Sauvignon Blanc, California's two most popular white wines, happily find a place in the early stages of a meal as well.

California's renown also make a spirited but low array of vermouths and sherries. Both red sweet vermouth and white dry vermouth on the rocks with a twist of lemon are surprisingly delicious introductions to dinner. The bright fruit flavors of the wines are echoed with hints of herbs and spice.

2

DEAN & DELUCA

APPETIZERS

CHAPTER 3

3

Organizations with values make valuable partners.

And people make the organization.

4

SYNERGY
IS A BEAUTIFUL THING.

5

1 The small photographs combine well with the copy.

2 Realism is a major factor in using photography, particularly for subjects such as food.

3 Good colour photography can really enhance the subject, producing an appealing image while reflecting the contents.

4 An interesting use of different sizes of image adds visual impact to this design.

5 An imaginative photograph can enhance any design and increase the visual appeal, as in this sales brochure.

It is very rare for photographs to be used exactly as they were taken. For one thing, if you are using photographs that were taken in different formats, it may not be possible to devise a grid that suits them all. For another, photographs often contain details that distract from the main subject. You will usually need to crop photographs.

Photography
Cropping and sizing

How to go about it

Construct a grid (see page 30) that will suit the majority of your images. This will give you initial ideas about the shape, size and composition of your images. Photographs should take up whole units of the grid in order to create a balanced and harmonious composition.

Cropping makes a vital difference to how a photograph is perceived. A good starting point is to decide on the main subject and make it as big as possible by taking away any irrelevant parts. Once you've cropped out the bits that you want to get rid of, enlarge the photographs to fit the prescribed unit of the grid.

Design decisions 1 This photograph contains too much detail, which distracts the viewer from the main subject. **2** Cropping the photograph produces a much stronger image. **3–8** This sequence shows how a simple image can be transformed by cropping. **9** Background detail can spoil a photograph. **10** By closing in on a particular area of the picture, you can easily add drama. **11** Removing the background altogether, leaving just the main subject, can greatly improve the image, particularly where portraits are concerned. (This is known as a cut-out.)

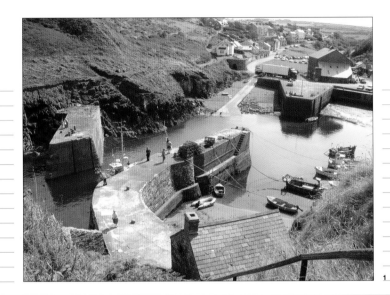

1

2

3

4

5

6

7

8

9

10

11

Exercise 35

- Select an action photograph that contains some people.
- Choose a suitable format and reproduce it without cropping.
- Now produce a sequence in which you gradually reduce the number of people in the image, finishing up with a single person.

Exercise 36

- Take a family photograph that includes a few people and reproduce it in a suitable shape, keeping all background detail.
- Next, crop the picture so the people are as large as possible. Make the people the focal point but keep in some of the background detail.
- Produce the same image, this time as a cut-out.

1

2

1 **The cropping creates different visual 'stories' for each of the photographs.**

2 **Focus is an important element of photography**

3 **Contrast in image size always creates mood and draws the eye into the picture.**

4 **Montaging photographs can demonstrate imaginative and interesting designs. The cut-out shapes give a dynamic feel to the piece.**

3

4

When you combine type and images, there is a natural temptation to overprint the text on the picture. More often than not, this interferes with the image. As a basic rule, keep text away from the image – or at least from the most important parts of it.

Text and images
Combining

Mood and position

Always try to choose a typeface that matches the mood of the picture. For example, an aggressive or powerful image might need a bold sans serif typeface. Conversely, a softer image would be enhanced by a lighter, more delicate type, a serif italic typeface such as Garamond or Caslon, for example.

Where you position the type is critical. Analyse the image carefully and look for elements within it to give a hint of how the type can be arranged.

Design decisions **1** The main subject of the image will contain certain angles and directions that you could echo in the type. **2** Having the image and type at contrasting angles or directions can create a more dynamic layout. **3** The content of the image may dictate how large or small it should be in relation to the text. **4** Is the text more important, or the image? **5** If space is tight, you may have to overprint the text on the image. Make sure the text does not interfere with the content of the image or obscure a critical part of it.

Offices are available in this modern, sophisticated office block recently redeveloped in the heart of the city.

the future is bright

1

**the future
is bright**

Offices are available in this modern, sophisticated office block recently redeveloped in the heart of the city.

2

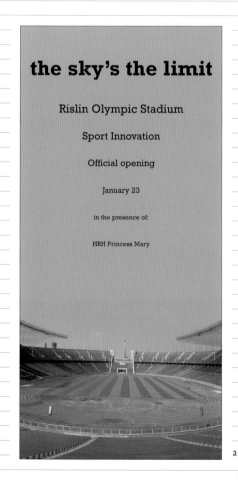

the sky's the limit

Rislin Olympic Stadium

Sport Innovation

Official opening

January 23

in the presence of:

HRH Princess Mary

3

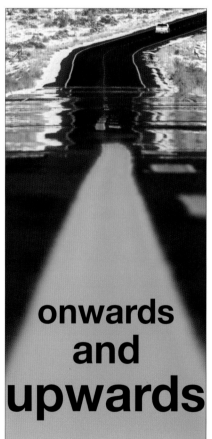

**onwards
and
upwards**

4

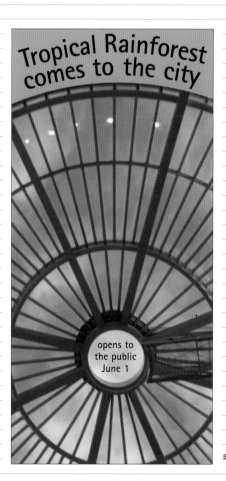

**Tropical Rainforest
comes to the city**

opens to
the public
June 1

5

Exercise 37

- Using an A4 format, select an action photograph and write a heading and a descriptive piece of text.
- Combine text and photograph with no contrast in direction.

Reach for the Skies

Just about any competent skater should be able to learn this trick in a month or two. It takes a while to learn the necessary coordination, but after that it is just a matter of practise. Keep your confidence, practise the move every time you go out skating and you will improve. Don't sweat about falling over: falling is a part of skating, and most likely you're not pushing your abilities if you're not taking a tumble once in a while. Stick with it and pretty soon you'll be flying with the birds – it's a wicked feeling and one worth all your effort. Go for it!

Exercise 38

- Using the photograph and text from exercise 37, position the heading and main text so that they run in a different direction to the image.
- Choose a different photograph, heading and text. Use a sans serif typeface. Set them so that the typeface, text, photograph and direction harmonise.

- Repeat this exercise, matching a sans serif typeface to the feeling the photograph gives.

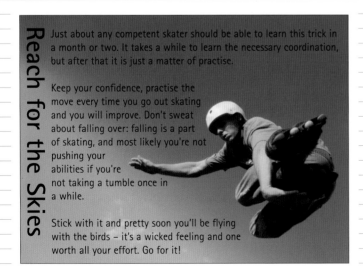

Reach for the Skies

Just about any competent skater should be able to learn this trick in a month or two. It takes a while to learn the necessary coordination, but after that it is just a matter of practise.

Keep your confidence, practise the move every time you go out skating and you will improve. Don't sweat about falling over: falling is a part of skating, and most likely you're not pushing your abilities if you're not taking a tumble once in a while.

Stick with it and pretty soon you'll be flying with the birds – it's a wicked feeling and one worth all your effort. Go for it!

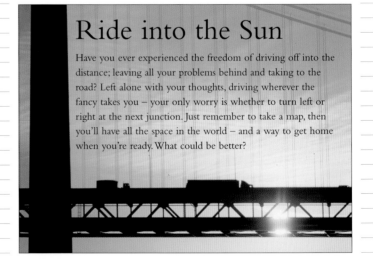

Ride into the Sun

Have you ever experienced the freedom of driving off into the distance; leaving all your problems behind and taking to the road? Left alone with your thoughts, driving wherever the fancy takes you – your only worry is whether to turn left or right at the next junction. Just remember to take a map, then you'll have all the space in the world – and a way to get home when you're ready. What could be better?

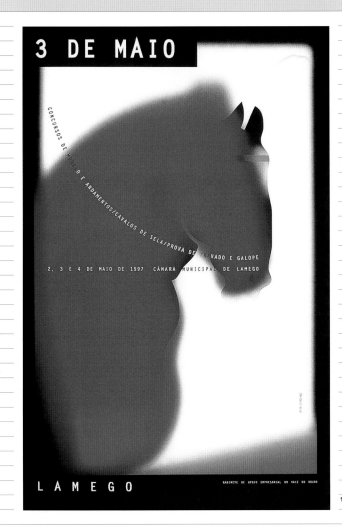

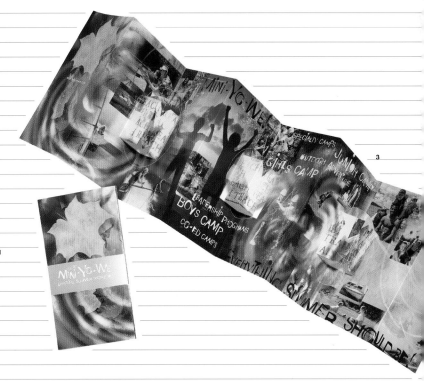

1 The shape of the small text carries the eye to the central point of the image. All other elements lie outside the image box, so this excellent poster is at once eye catching and very clear.

2 Interesting juxtaposition of image and ornament. The lettering on the image has been placed so as not to interfere with the photograph.

3 The energetic, colourful way the imagery and text have been designed perfectly reflects the content.

two magpies = 雙喜 double

happiness (*shuāng xǐ*)

眞顏 ● 人們相喜悅為報喜之鳥。一夫妻時代，人們認為前後互有連繫喜事的報喜。可禮之前二作人，皆喜成好的歡呼，聲音說是在好事之旅。人佛像上拈花，約歡呼因为，一喜侧音喜喜在喜喜喜喜報果真喜。真喜的雙喜成—喜明喜喜成喜喜喜的歡果真分喜喜喜喜，破離題喜小喜題，一人喜妻分之旬子和私—喜別喜喜之喜就曾喜，一人喜有以喜報果真喜喜果的百前。

magpie / The characters for 'magpie,' *xǐ què*, literally mean the 'bird of happiness.' A picture of two magpies facing each other stands for 'double happiness,' *shuāng xǐ*, symbolic of conjugal bliss. The call of a magpie foretells the arrival of a guest, good news, or good fortune. A magpie resting on a plum branch conveys the wish 'happiness before one's brow,' *xǐ shàng méi shāo*, as the word for 'plum' and 'brow'

are both pronounced *méi*. Magpies also served to preserve the integrity of a marriage, according to legend. When a husband and wife were to be apart for any reason, they would break a mirror and each take half. If the wife was unfaithful, her half of the mirror turned into a magpie that flew back and informed her husband. Consequently, an image of a magpie is often placed on the back of a mirror.

double happiness ● 171

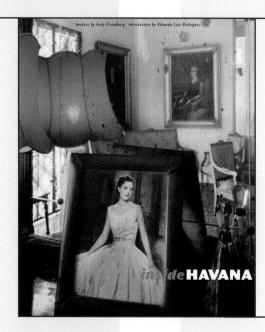

preface by *Andy Grundberg*   introduction by *Eduardo Luis Rodríguez*

inside**HAVANA**

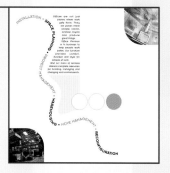

Section Two

Design Projects and Categories

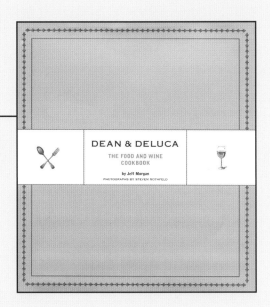

Now that you have been introduced to the basic theory of design, it is time to put your ideas and knowledge into practice.

Whatever you're working on, every design project falls into three distinct phases. The first is the brief, where you establish with the client what the aims and objectives of the project are. The second phase is thinking up the design itself – drawing thumbnails of your ideas is likely to help clarify your thought processes. The third phase is the production of the design, and here discussion between the designer and the production team is just as important as that between the designer and the client.

This section is concerned primarily with the second phase – the creative stage. Design projects fall into a number of different categories, each with its own requirements. The following pages examine some of these areas and illustrate the processes involved with case studies and professional examples. There are also exercises for you to develop your design and self-assessment skills as you build up your knowledge bank and gain the confidence you need to become an innovative and exciting designer.

Whether you are being briefed by someone else or are setting your own brief, certain questions arise at the outset of any design project that form the basis of the discussion between you and the client. In today's language, these questions might be expressed as 'www.h' – why, what, when and how much?

Briefs

W – why is it needed?

This should clarify the purpose of the project (for example, are you producing a marketing tool to sell a specific product, or an informational piece?) and the market you are aiming at. Once this has been established, you and the client can decide what specialisms are required and set other processes, such as research and marketing, in motion.

W – what do you intend to do?

This defines how you will meet the aims. What type of design and visual approach will suit the purpose? Will it be print- or screen-based or a mix of both? What kind of visual research is required? Are photographers, illustrators or copywriters needed?

W – when is it needed?

The deadline will determine the schedule for design and production. All three partners in the project – client, designer and production team – should be aware of the schedule and the dates agreed for the delivery of the items. The client will be responsible for the budget, text and aims; the designer for the visual aspects and the technical proficiency of the design; and the production team for ensuring that the project is finished on time and to the specifications required. It is the designer who negotiates between the client and the production team.

H – how much is the budget?

It is rare for a budget to be unlimited, and the amount of money allocated to the project will set the parameters for both you, as the designer, and the production team. Generous budgets give you the freedom to explore the use of extra colours or ancillary processes such as lamination, varnishing, embossing or cut-outs. However, a limited budget does not necessarily mean a poor visual result: an imaginative designer and an enterprising production team can maximise limited budgets by clever use of colour, imposition, and so on. Good design is about using the resources you have to maximum effect.

At the briefing stage, you and the client are equally responsible for ensuring that you understand each other's thoughts and ideas: the client has to make it clear what he or she wants, and you have to make sure the client understands what you're proposing to do. Always make a written record of what has been agreed.

- You have been called in by a client to discuss an educational booklet to accompany two television series – *The Secrets of Sleep* and *In Your Dreams*. Both series explore the unconscious world of sleep.

- Draw up a list of the questions you should ask in order to ensure that your design meets the aims and objectives of the project.
- Now work with a colleague or friend who acts as the client. Discuss the project – making sure your questions are answered – and find out if the client has any specific requirements that you have not covered.

- Confirm in writing what has been agreed in the course of your discussions. Ask the client to do the same and compare your notes. Are there discrepancies?
- The ideas below will help you get started.

Brief for *The Secrets of Sleep* and *In Your Dreams*

W – Why is it needed?
1. What is the purpose of the booklet?
2. How closely will it be based on the television series?
3. Will it be published in more than one country?
4. Who is the target audience? Age group? Social group?

W – What do we intend to do?
1. How many pages are there?
2. What size is the booklet?
3. Will it be a four-colour print process?
4. Will it be illustrated with photographs and artworks?
5. Will there be a lot of scientific cross-referencing? Should the design allow for footnotes or endnotes?

W – When is it needed?
1. Is there an interim date for roughs?
2. Is it expected at the printers on this date?
3. Is there any leeway on the deadline date?

H – How much is the budget?
1. Does this include the designer's expenses?
2. Does it include VAT?

Client's considerations

- Give the designer a general overview of the project: it's an educational booklet aimed at the general public, age group 30-40, no specialised knowledge of dreams. Each booklet will be:

  i)   32 pages
  ii) full colour throughout
  iii) portrait format
  iv) A5 format
  v)   perfect bound

- Discuss the budget. Will you offer a rejection fee? Expenses?
- Discuss payment and contract terms, for example, would the designer like payment in stages or once the job is complete?
- Discuss photographers and illustrators, the designer is responsible for commissioning where necessary. Discuss how many images per double page spread.
- Discuss a schedule. When will the material be ready to send to the designer? How long before the layouts have to be fully finalised and approved?
- If the designer does not meet deadlines, will there be a reduction in the fee?
- Tell the designer what kind of presentation you expect, for example, do you need colour laser proofs or black and white? How many sets of proofs do you need? Who will handle production?

Logos range from abstract and illustrative marks to letterforms that clearly identify the subject. Some logos are purely abstract and illustrative, for example, the Shell logo. Strictly speaking, however, logotype refers to a letterform – and this is what we consider in this section.

Logos & Stationery

Logos

There are three criteria for successful logotypes: 1. The design should reflect the nature of the organisation. 2. The logo should be compact and distinctive. 3. It should work in a single colour as well as in full colour, and should reproduce adequately at various sizes, from the very small (business card) to the extremely large (banners and posters).

In some ways, it is better to start your design of a logo in black and white. Don't forget that you have tones to work with, which gives a good range of greys. You can easily add colour later once you are satisfied with the black-and-white version.

The letterform you choose will depend on the feel you wish to impart. Once you have made your choice, you need to look at how the letters fit together. The best technique is to set the logotype in your preferred type and then experiment with kerning so that the combinations of letters that make up the logo look visually balanced. You may have to reform some letters to achieve this, but do not take away too much of the type, as this may result in illegible or visually impaired forms.

To begin with, put the letterforms in simple shapes – a square, circle or triangle. Work with black letters about 2.5cm high on a white ground. Then you might try reversing from positive to negative. Perhaps try partially removing the background shape. The lessons you learned earlier concerning type selection, reversing out and colour usage will apply.

Stationery

Once you have designed your logo, you need to apply it to stationery items – primarily a letterhead, compliments slip and business card. Start with the letterhead, as this will set the style for the other items. It is a good idea to collect letters from a number of different companies and file them for future reference.

Letterheads nearly always follow standard sizes. A letter is normally folded twice to fit into an envelope, so think of it in three parts. The top third will contain the company's logo, its name and address and the address of the recipient. These elements need to balance with each other. You also need to make sure that nothing important sits on the fold. A good solution is for the addressee to be on the left (in fact, this is essential if window envelopes are to be used). The logo should be positioned so that it harmonises with the address panel, although the exact position will depend on the overall feel you wish to impart.

You should also discuss with the client which typefaces will suit the letterhead. If much additional information has to be incorporated (different branches or a list of officers of the company, for example), this can be accommodated at the foot of the letter or to one side. Finally, remember that space must be left if letters are to be filed and holes punched.

Ancillary processes, such as foil printing (metallic material printed onto an image), die-stamping (raised surfaces in gloss or matt inks) or blind embossing or debossing (indentations into or out of the paper stock) can also be exploited on stationery.

- Produce a series of design development sheets containing ideas for a logotype design, choosing one of the following companies for your project:

  Smell Sensation – a chain of florists competing in the same market as Interflora.

  Optimum – a camera and optics manufacturer producing quality compact SLR cameras to compete with Canon and Nikon.

  Giacometti – an Italian restaurant serving traditional Italian food, which wants a modern feel.

- The logo should reflect the products or service and personality of the company. Restrict yourself to letterforms and basic shapes – do not add any other visual material. Annotate your designs with written comments explaining how you developed your ideas and evaluating their potential.

- Apply the logo to a letterhead, business card and compliments slip. Add an address. Try various options, then print them out and decide which work best.

- The ideas below will help you get started.

Optimum

Optimum

Optimum

Optimum

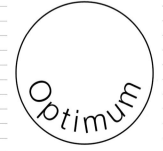

Optimum

Optimum

Optimum

Optimum

Optimum

Optimum

The two case studies shown here conform very well to the criteria set out on pages 90–91. Both have distinctive features that visually reflect the character of the organisation. Both are shown in black and white, which means they can easily be used for a variety of purposes, such as photocopying and faxing.

Logos & Stationery

Case Studies

The Teatro Bruto design reflects the client's approach to their theatrical projects. Bruto means raw and unpolished, and the theatre company's projects are experimental but professional in nature. Rubber-stamp letters applied with varying degrees of pressure were used to convey a rough, imperfect feel and the resulting effect was then created digitally for the logo.

The Estudio de Opera do Porto provides a link between conservatoire studies and professional work for the most promising singers. Its logo uses the letter 'o' to represent the open mouth of a singer, while the quotation marks are a reference to the other important element in opera, the libretto, or text.

1 The starting point is experimentation with various letterforms and colours to find which one can be best translated onto a rubber stamp.
2 Close up, the individual letters illustrate how much ink is lost in the stamping process. For this reason, a precise, clean sans serif is used so that parts of characters can be dropped without affecting legibility.
3 The result is a visually exciting logo that accurately reflects the client's business.

1

2

3

Professional Examples

4 The quotation marks are satisfyingly heavy and securely bracket the O, so that this is delineated from the rest of the logo and does not merge into or become confused with the rest of the copy.

5 The condensed sans serif typeface represents the shape of a singing mouth as well as being the Portuguese for 'the'.

6 This copy clearly conveys the information of the logo.

7 The result is a reasonably complex and sophisticated logo, with three elements that work in harmony to cleverly and simply describe the business.

4

5

**ESTÚDIO
DE ÓPERA
DO PORTO**
CASA DA MÚSICA

6

8

TEAO🌿GY

9

10

11

"O ESTÚDIO
DE ÓPERA
DO PORTO
CASA DA MÚSICA **"**

7

8 The identity highlights three elements: the global, the digital and the bold initial letter of 'Allavida', reflecting the style and focus of the organisation.

9 This 'no fuss' black logo has been designed for a producer of healthy teas. Adding the graphic shape of a tea leaf to the letter L creates the concept for this logo.

10 The logo has been designed 'signature-style' for an art gallery. The name of the gallery in freehand, the 'typed' address and the unusual format combine to convey the idea of artistic freedom and creativity.

11 The logotype, spelling OVA, uses graphic forms created from a fragmented and textured image to suggest different contexts.

A newsletter is something of a hybrid between a magazine and a newspaper. Published by large- or medium-sized companies, clubs and leisure organisations, it provides a platform for news, social activities, staff movements and general activities within the organisation.

Newsletter

Generally, newsletters do not have the urgency that accompanies newspapers or magazines and the extra time can allow you scope to implement some good ideas. The design decisions follow a pattern. First, the budget. Maybe only one colour is available for the main content, although two might be used for the cover. With constraints such as this, use display type, rules and tints to give variety to backgrounds. If two colours are available on the front and back cover, then you can use duotones for the photographs and the second colour for the title and main headings.

The next decision concerns the format. This may be influenced by logistical considerations (for example, the need to fit the newsletter into a standard-sized envelope, or to keep it lightweight so that postage costs are not excessive), and the amount of text to be incorporated. Cramming in too much text is visually off-putting for the reader; try to keep a generous amount of white space and to bring visual variety to the pages by changing the picture sizes and using displayed headings. If there is a lot of text and the number of pages cannot be increased, use small text sizes in sans serif or narrow-set types to help you to fit in the copy.

The first priority in designing a newsletter is to analyse the copy. Break it into sections – features, news, sport, staff movements, and so on. This will give you a good guide as to the kind of grid you should construct. Features might use wide columns whereas news items, sports results or staff movements would be better suited to narrower columns.

Once you have completed the grid, try it out with the different sections of copy. Rules and display type can help divide up sections and they offer visual clarity to the page. In your text selection, follow the principles set out in Section 1. You can emphasise items by changing the typeface or the form (from roman to italic, for example), and by introducing panels

and colour. The overall style should reflect the organisation's view of itself – modern and trendy, or conservative and traditional, for example:

Once you have established the grid and overall style, set up style sheets for future issues. The company may want to produce subsequent issues itself, in which case, your role will be in a supervisory and advisory capacity. If the style sheets are comprehensive, visual problems can be kept to a minimum.

appearance   appearance

appearance
summer
issue

appearance
summer issue

- You have been asked to produce ideas for a newsletter for a firm of land developers. The company's services cover architecture, building and construction, interior design and landscape gardening. The newsletter is to be called *Appearance* and the target audience is between the ages of 25 and 40. The newsletter should look very modern.

- Design a front cover with the masthead and the copy 'Summer Issue'.
- Source suitable photographs and design a double-page spread containing a feature article with appropriate sub-headings.
- Design another spread with text about staff leaving and joining the company. Small photos of the personnel can be used. Make up some copy on forthcoming projects.

- Ask a colleague to analyse your efforts and discuss the strengths and weaknesses of the design.
- The ideas below will help you get started.

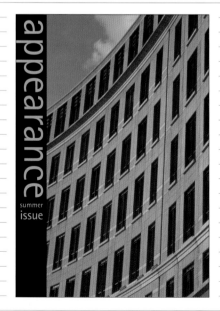

Sometimes you can afford to be brave and experimental in designing a
newsletter, but of course this depends very much on what the client wants.
The style should reflect how the organisation in question perceives itself; how
much information they want to convey and what their budget is.

Newsletter

Case Studies

This newsletter is exclusive to members of FÍT
– The Association of Icelandic Graphic
Designers. Its aim is to publish industry news
and announcements in an interesting and lively
fashion, and to this end the approach to layout
and typography breaks with tradition. The use
of flat colour, graphic shapes, space, type as
image and varying setting styles all combine to
give the design a dynamic thrust.

It is unusually adventurous to use only
typographic elements in a newsletter, but the
approach is successful in this instance
because it reflects the purpose of the
client's organisation.

1 **Notice how the type on the head runs both ways.**

2 **The use of rules is unusual and brave, but they work
well to balance and help push back the masthead.**

3 **The text acts as a texture, not as information.**

4 **A simple efficient design for a technical newsletter.**

5 **Coloured panels, changes in setting style and
breaking display type into short lines all combine to
make a lively spread.**

6 **This illustrates a very economic use of space – no
room is wasted on a masthead panel or wide
margins. The vertical setting of the masthead, its
cropping and right and left ranging mean it can
function as a rule delineating the text.**

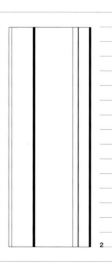

Professional Examples

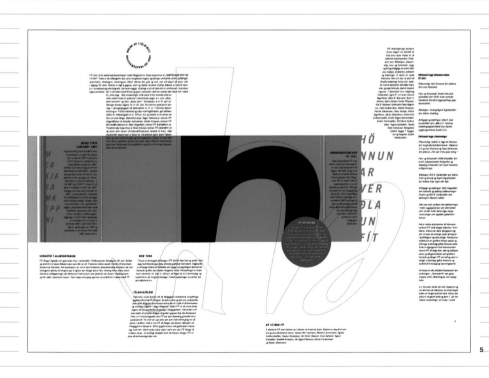

A brochure covers all kinds of sales literature and informative material, ranging from copy for art exhibitions, to health and safety issues. With so much variety, the public has come to expect visually exciting designs and the designer has to meet these expectations – although not at the expense of clarity.

Brochure

As with newsletters, the first step is to establish the grid by analysing the content. If the brochure is primarily a sales vehicle, then the emphasis will be on pictorial information (photographs and illustrations), with explanatory text playing a subsidiary role. The text might consist of little more than model numbers and prices or it might go into more detailed descriptions of the objects. If the text comprises both these elements then a flexible grid with small units would suit, as this gives you the chance to have a number of different column measures to encompass varying sizes of visual material and small blocks of text. Wider columns are better for more detailed, explanatory text.

In other types of brochure, the ratio of text to pictures may be more or less equal and therefore the grid can be less complex. Photographs need captions, and captions look much better on narrow measures, so allocate a small unit in the grid for this purpose.

Once you have decided on the grid and have received all the material from the client, try out several double-page spreads to see how the text (including captions) and photographs or illustrations fit in. You can quickly make adjustments on the basis of these trial compositions. Sometimes it's a good idea to show the client several versions of the same spread at the first presentation, as this can provide a good starting point for discussion.

Even if the brochure is primarily informative, with more text than pictures, try to change the 'pace' of the spreads. This can be difficult to achieve with the text, as you should avoid too many changes in type size or measure, but you should certainly aim for a contrast in the way you present the visual imagery. You can do this through size (with large pictures set against smaller, more detailed ones) or colour (by including black-and-white images amongst ones that are predominantly four-colour or juxtaposing four-colour images with duotones). The treatment of the picture material also calls for skills in cropping (see pages 78–79). The ability to compose spreads with visual interest and at the same time not overdo the 'fireworks' is the essence of good brochure design.

- Design three black-and-white double-page spreads for a brochure to accompany a photographic exhibition. Use at least eight photographs over the three spreads.
- Write a suitable caption for each photograph.
- Then design the cover and add a suitable title and image.
- With a colleague, analyse the result and discuss the strengths and weaknesses of the design.
- The ideas below will help you get started.

Places of Culture

Around the world
in eighty pages

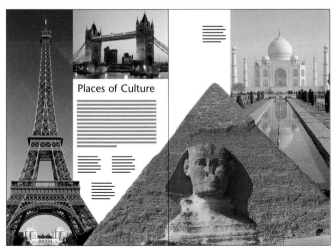

Places of Culture

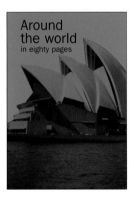

Around
the world
in eighty pages

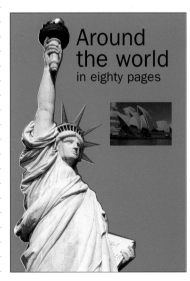

Around
the world
in eighty pages

Sales brochures need to be colourful and imaginative. This spread, from a
brochure promoting a company that offers quality workflow solutions, is a good
example of the integration of image and text. The copy line 'efficient' is
reinforced by choosing the epitome of efficiency – a clock – as the image.

Brochure

Case Study

The composition of this spread is attractive.
There is a high degree of contrast between the
pages – one side presents the text while the other
is dominated by the graphic image. The use of
white space is generous, allowing the eye to
wander over the different types of information.

This text is imaginatively typeset with various
measures, sizes and setting styles. Range left
and justified settings have all been employed to
good effect – the end result is attractive and
not overcomplicated.

1 **The conventional range-left main text and
subheadings convey the information in a very clear
and sensible manner. This balances the effect of
sophisticated imagery and prevents the spread
looking overworked.**

2 **An interesting use of text as image. Repeating the
copy and showing much less text above the 'in'
tray than above the 'out' tray reinforces the sales
message of efficiency and productivity.**

3 **A segment of the stopwatch has been pulled into
the right-hand page. This serves two purposes:
first, the segment acts as a rule on which to place
the word 'efficient' (and how apposite that a
segment of a stopwatch, itself illustrating a clock,
is the rule). Second, the white space it leaves gives
some relief on this high-impact page; conversely,
the segment on the right-hand page fills what
would otherwise have been empty space.**

Professional Examples

4

5

6

4 The interest in this design lies in the wide top and bottom margins and the thick vertical rules acting as right and left margins and separating the text from the photograph. The figure appears to be centred in the photograph, although this is a false effect as the image stretches over the gutter into the right page.

5 There is a good balance on this brochure cover, with lively integration of shapes and images.

6 The text image draws attention immediately because of the angle at which it is set. The photograph is well placed on the text, giving it a three-dimensional effect and endowing the cover with a sense of unity.

7 The double-page spread appears slightly eerie – an effect achieved by the use of a limited number of deep colours. The masthead is emphasised and drawn out of the page by the red panel.

Burials, buckets and beyond . . .

7

There is probably more variety in the world of magazines than in any other category of design. Magazines range from the serious and informative to the frivolous and satirical, and cover almost every subject imaginable.

Magazine

As with newsletters and brochures, you need to analyse the target audience and the aims of the magazine before you embark on the design as different kinds of magazine require different visual treatment. The content will determine the grid: some magazine grids (mostly for magazines that have a high text content) are closely structured, while others (where the emphasis is on pictorial elements) are much freer.

The client's contribution is more important to the success of a magazine than it is in the other categories we have covered, for it is the material that the client provides, both visual and textual, that influences the way the pages look. The look and feel depend ultimately on what the client wants. Serious academic magazines, for example, are generally text oriented, so you should concentrate on establishing legible sizes of type with good leading and type measures that do not result in too many word breaks. It may be preferable to use a serif type to give the magazine a serious, more traditional feel. Sans serif headings as a contrast will give an air of modernity.

Readers tend to dip into magazines, rather than read the whole magazine from cover to cover, which is why it is important to have plenty of visual interest. Try to create changes of 'pace' – which means that if one spread is quiet and textual, the next one should be much more visual. As a starting point, look at the wealth of magazines on the market for ideas to suit particular needs. Well designed examples will demonstrate how image and type can be integrated dynamically.

- You have been invited to pitch for the redesign of an arts magazine, the title of which you need to choose from the following: Art Now, Contemporary Art, Articulate or Artworks. The main feature is on the artist, Alec Hunting.

- Design a masthead, using your chosen title.
- Then design a front cover incorporating the masthead with the following copy:
  Hunting at the Central Gallery
  pop art or minimalism?
  Ends May 31

- Construct a grid of five or six columns, then choose a maximum of three fonts that you can use for the text, quotations, parts of the copy that can be displayed within the text, headlines and captions.
- Design at least two double-page spreads on Alec Hunting (or an art subject of your choice). Concentrate on the pace of the article, alternating the ratios of text to image over the two spreads.
- The ideas below will help you get started.

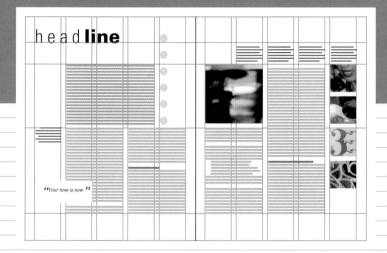

Magazine

Case Study

The British Film Institute publishes *Sight and Sound*. Updating the style of the magazine to keep abreast with design innovations and new technology is of premium importance for such a long-running and successful magazine. The most recent redesign has introduced interesting new features.

1 **The modern, sans serif typeface is called Bruener. The small ampersand has been made bolder so that it matches the weight of the rest of the masthead.**

2 **The heads are always written in a sans serif typeface, giving a modern, trendy feel to the magazine. Legibility is not compromised as running text is written in a serif typeface.**

3 **Magazine design thrives on visual change and panels of colour are one way to achieve this. They also give the page a structure and serve to differentiate items. The magazine manages to include all production details of every film it reviews by setting the type very small and with two narrow columns within the grid unit – this is an extremely efficient use of space.**

4 **This double-page spread shows plenty of visual interest. Contrasts in picture size, the use of coloured panels and a flexible use of the grid are all good practice in magazine design.**

5 **The display type demonstrates a good use of vertical alignment. The thick rule provides a balance in weight.**

6 Insetting the display quote in the text retains the column structure and emphasises the copy. Contrast in typestyle (here from bold sans serif to serif) is good practice for caption setting.

Sight&Sound

The Monthly Film Magazine/November 2002/£3.25

1

Interview

Premium Bond

Edward Lawrenson: Were you surprised when you got the call to do the movie?
Lee Tamahori: I was, because I thought I'd have been the last person they'd ask. I was doing another hard-edged, visceral movie in LA which had just fallen apart. My agent phoned and I didn't hesitate. First, I wanted to do a movie my kids could watch because

2

Two Men Went to War

United Kingdom 2002

Director	**Music Supervisor**
John Henderson	Robin Morrison
Producers	**Music Producer**
Ira Trattner	Michael Paert
Pat Harding	**Production Co-ordinator**
Screenplay	Claire Griffin
Richard Everett	**Executive Producer**
Christopher Villiers	Tony Prior
Director of Photography	Fireworks Music Ltd
John Ignatius	**Music Editor**
Editor	Michael Paert
David Yardley	**Music Recordist/Mixer**
Production Designers	Gerry O'Riordan
Sophie Becher	**Soundtrack**
Steve Carter	"Run, Rabbit,Run", "(We're
Music/Music Conductor	Gonna Hang Out) The
Richard Harvey	Washing on the Siegfried
	Line" – Flanagan and
	Allen; "Turn Your Money
©Two Men Went to War	in Your Pocket" – Jimmy
Partnership	

3

little dangerous handing out guns in a bank?" asks Moore.

After this things dip slightly, with Moore going for a soft target, the Michigan Militia. At one of their meetings, a shooter – a real-estate negotiator when not in fatigues – asks Moore. "Who's going to defend your kids? The cops? The Federal Government?" Moore raises his eyebrows and plays to the gallery with a lame joke. "Do you take one of these guns with you when you're negotiating real-estate?"

It's a rare low point. The Michigan Militia was created in the wake of the Ruby Ridge massacre in Idaho in 1992. At Ruby Ridge a young boy and his mother – who was armed only with an 18-month-old baby – were murdered by Federal snipers in a bungled and wholly inappropriate raid on a peaceful (if slightly paranoid) white separatist family.

"Had we cruelly trampled the purveyors of documentary truth in our rush to the top?"

The exact same snipers committed a similar atrocity a few months later at Waco, Texas.

Sir the Michigan Militia's concerns about the Federal Government deserve to be treated with something other than arched eyebrows. The Weaver family at Ruby Ridge and David Koresh's parishioners at Waco were victims of liberal America – gunned down because their peaceful, if odd, beliefs didn't fit the prevailing norm. Moore ought to be championing these underdogs in the same way he champions victims of corporate globalisation, but he doesn't. They are, to him, just wackos. Indeed later in the film he includes a clip or two of the protesters who gathered at Ruby Ridge to support the Weaver family. Again he portrays them simply as gun nuts, without contextualising the cause of their anger. As Randy Weaver once said to me, "Clinton bombed some country the name of which he couldn't in the US could pronounce", he asks, what is it about America that produces so much gun violence?

ourselves in the Rose McElveen arts March, top; Nick Jame's Biggie and

Tupac, centre; the Maysles brothers with Mick Jagger in 1970's 'Gimme Shelter', above; Joe Ranson, below

opened at Columbine is a microcosm of what on throughout the world." It's as if this represents sees himself as a bystander to these mail-supposed to being at their very heart.

tone is a superb polemicist, Chomsky with a brilliant collage of both kitsch archive material polemics. After an opening moral har documents America's obsession guns throughout its cultural and cal history, he is seen walking into Sweeten bank. "I want the account can get the free gun." he says. The manager unblinkingly agrees only prerequisite to this offer quaintly, that the account isn't "criminally defective" is OK if I'm normally nefective but not criminally." Moore. "Yes," says the bank ger "Don't you think it's a

was nobody blaming bowling? In the aftermath of Columbine children were expelled from schools across the US, one for painting a chicken drumstick as a teacher. "Yes, our children were indeed something to fear," says Moore.

Ultimately *Bowling for Columbine* is a film about the way Americans are fear junkies and the media provides all the fear they want. Fear of Marilyn Manson, fear of out-of-control children, and – post 11 September – fear of everything, which sanctions US foreign-policy outrages. In grappling with this concept, Moore transforms himself from a political commentator into a philosophical one. His suggestion is that the fostering of fear is a capitalist sleight of hand designed to deflect Americans' attention from the things they should be angry about – the things that make money for corporations.

"A country that's this out of control with fear shouldn't have all those guns and ammo lying about." Moore con-

"Broomfield and I also arch our eyebrows at neo-Nazis, but I'm trying to stop doing this"

Arms and a man in investigating US attitudes to guns in 'Bowling for Columbine', Moore, above; Martin, top, among others

draws statements from a representative of arms manufacturer Lockheed Martin, top, among others

cludes, ending the film by going after the National Rifle Association president Charlton Heston. It's a disappointing climax, which attempts to ape his debut *Roger & Me*. But Roger Smith was a worthy target, and Heston is not. Sure, Heston was a little foolish in holding an NRA meeting down the street from Columbine High a few days after the massacre. But he's a lobbyist who's not responsible for the murders of little girls, and when Moore leaves a framed photograph of a murdered little girl on Heston's doorstep and wanders away with his head bowed, the pathos backfires. In demonising the NRA – he even accuses them of being the Ku Klux Klan by another name – Moore is himself guilty of inappropriate scaremongering. It's an unsatisfactory ending to an otherwise brilliant documentary.

'Bowling for Columbine' is showing on 10 and 11 November at the NFT, is released on 15 November and is reviewed on page 40. For details of the RLFF programme call 020 7928 3232 or visit www.rlff.com

Detailed: Audrey Tautou as Senay

Nick James on Stephen Frears' London immigrant drama

Subterranean homesick blues

Given how unwittily Stephen Frears seems to be able to hop from US-based movies like 'The Grifters' (1990) and 'High Fidelity' (2000) to British-scale features from 'My Beautiful Laundrette' (1985) to 'Liam' (2000), it ought not to be such a surprise to find him portraying the hidden workers of London. Yet 'Dirty Pretty Things' is startling in the current climate because it's so unafraid of qualities which script-formula genre advise against. It's a sunny urban thriller with an obvious spatial effects and a weighty political dimension. It stars a little-known male lead in Chiwetel Ejiofor (admittedly playing opposite such European stars as Audrey 'Amélie' Tautou and Sergi López) and is set in a downbeat milieu of the dispossessed, filmed with appropriate tension and bleakness by Chris Menges.

Okwe (Ejiofor) is a Nigerian man, once a doctor but now ducking sleep to pull wraps on two low-paid posts in London – nightman at the seedy Baltic hotel and daytime minicab driver – with a further sideline in ministering to the STDs of his equally 'stateless' colleagues. He sleeps on a couch

belonging to one of the Baltic's cleaners Senay (Tautou), a Turkish immigrant working illegally. When the attentions of the immigration inspectors force her out of her job, she's ripe for victimisation. Okwe feels responsible for her but seems powerless to help. Soon they are caught at the rim of a vicious whirlpool of deprivation.

The sense of a class of workers invisible to the citizens they serve lies dependent on each other is deftly achieved. But you shouldn't get the impression this is a worthy film. It's an effective thriller made all the more urgent by the social concerns at its heart, and its horrific elements are as uneasy and gripping as anything in 'The Grifters'. Some might find Tautou's inescapable cuteness a touch inappropriate at times, but she remains pleasingly brittle and holds her own among this terrific cast. Most of all it seems like a film that could have come from the heyday of 1960s television-financed film-making that we seem to have lost sight of recently – except that the issues it illustrates could not be more vital to the present. 'Dirty Pretty Things' is on 6 and 7 November

Doctor in the house: Chiwetel Ejiofor in Okwe

The main attraction

Ryan Gilbey wonders if the politics of 'Changing Lanes' are shift stick or unthinkingly automatic

Street legal

Reviews

Samuel L. Jackson has not yet provided compelling evidence that he can play much besides funky hipsters (*Pulp Fiction, The Long Kiss Goodnight*) or righteous avengers (*A Time to Kill*), but the conscientious thriller *Changing Lanes* hints there are fresh ambiguities to be mined in the latter category. Here Jackson plays Doyle Gipson, whose abstinence from alcohol does little to temper his temper after a collision on New York's FDR Drive with hotshot attorney Gavin Banek (Ben Affleck). Doyle tries to act honourably. It is he who refuses Gavin's offer of a blank cheque, and later he will also make an attempt to return to Gavin the important legal

both instances Doyle's good nature goes unappreciated. In the first Gavin speeds off to court, leaving Doyle – who also has a court appointment, to stop his ex-wife and young sons from moving state – stranded on the freeway. In the second Doyle's altruism comes too late to prevent Gavin's visit to Mr Finch, a computer hacker who renders Doyle bankrupt with the touch of a button.

The screenplay, by Michael Tolkin (*The Player, Deep Cover*) and debutant Chap Taylor, sometimes seems poised to commit the ultimate heresy of making a main character in a Hollywood movie unsympathetic: in one scene Doyle clubs two casually racist strangers with

Theroux and I never hug, though Broomfield recently became a neo-hugger (see the final "you make a lovely stew" scene in *Biggie and Tupac*).

At his very best, in *Roger & Me* and now *Bowling for Columbine*, Moore is quite brilliant at creating – using archive material and savage comedy – a political panorama that startlingly interweaves the macro with the micro. One of the most powerful and convincing moments in *Bowling for Columbine* is his drawing of a parallel between the US selling weaponry to Eric Harris and Dylan Klebold, the teenagers who shot up Columbine High on 20 April 1999, and the US providing training and finance to Osama Bin Laden during Russia's invasion of Afghanistan. He even manages to get a representative of arms manufacturer Lockheed Martin to say, "What ▶

"I want the account where I get a free gun, says Moore. The bank manager calmly agrees"

In some respects, advertising is different to the other categories of design as it uses a hard-sell approach to increase sales and persuade people to buy. However, the same general principles of good design apply.

Advertisements for Print

To a large extent, this type of advertising relies heavily on a combination of a strong concept and good art direction. Both the language and the imagery have to convince the audience that this product is for them. Good copywriting is essential: the copy has to register with the audience. In this scenario, your role as designer is to clarify the message through good typography and composition.

If the advertising is promotional or informative, you can play a more influential part. Once the copy has been written and the points of emphasis established, you can use visual ideas to reflect the content of the copy.

Our culture has promoted the expectation that advertisements should be visually different, and this offers you the chance to be more adventurous in your composition and use of type. Dynamic use of imagery allied to imaginative typography can result in advertisements that get noticed. If the design is to rely solely on copy without imagery, then negative leading, overlapping of type, changing the direction of type and visual experimentation can provide the solution to the problem. The copy can also be written in such a way as to allow you to exploit humour through your choice and placement of type. As with all things, there is a limit as to how far you should go with 'wacky' typefaces, but advertising is one category in which you can afford to experiment.

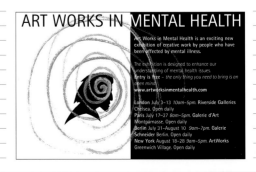

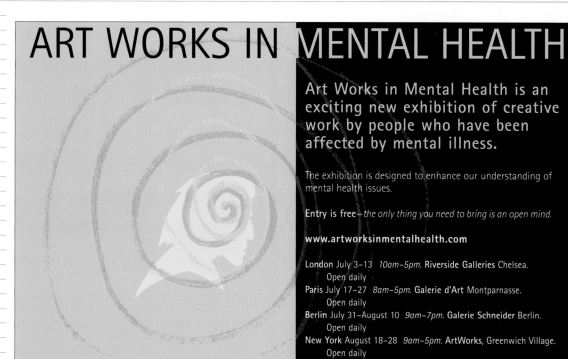

ART WORKS IN MENTAL HEALTH

Art Works in Mental Health is an exciting new exhibition of creative work by people who have been affected by mental illness.

The exhibition is designed to enhance our understanding of mental health issues.

Entry is free—*the only thing you need to bring is an open mind.*

www.artworksinmentalhealth.com

London July 3–13 *10am–5pm*. **Riverside Galleries** Chelsea.
  Open daily
Paris July 17–27 *8am–5pm*. **Galerie d'Art** Montparnasse.
  Open daily
Berlin July 31–August 10 *9am–7pm*. **Galerie Schneider** Berlin.
  Open daily
New York August 18–28 *9am–5pm*. **ArtWorks**, Greenwich Village.
  Open daily

Advertisements for Print

Case Study

The design features that link the advertisements are the uniform basic shape, the eye-catching signature 'garbs' and the store details. These combine to make the series instantly recognisable and, most importantly, memorable.

An interesting feature is the way the advertisements exploit well-known phrases by using ones with similar sounds and meanings to refer to the products: for example, in the advert for the bag, we see 'stuff' instead of 'staff'.

The typography used is simple yet it demonstrates variety. Different use of capitals and lower case letters, typefaces and punctuation all add to the impact. The weight of the type evokes the feel of the products: medium-weight type for the boots and bag, a bold condensed form for the sweaters and heavy-weight type for the coats.

1 **A good choice of type sizes for the main heading that gives a balanced feel. A direct visual link between different sizes and styles is made through the use of the ruler.**

2–3 **The label, naming the designer of the bag, is added as a style feature. The centred copy under the main image means that symmetry is possible in the main body of this neat advertisement.**

4 **The image has a three-dimensional appearance but retains its simplicity through the device of having a dark sweater at the top of the pile and a light one immediately underneath.**

5 **Using an ampersand in a different colour to the rest of the main heading means that a lot of characters can fit on the line in a large type, without appearing cramped. The heading aligns exactly with the central image.**

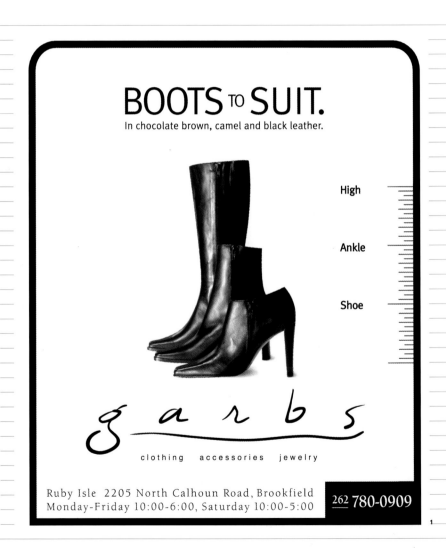

BOOTS TO SUIT.

In chocolate brown, camel and black leather.

High

Ankle

Shoe

garbs

clothing   accessories   jewelry

Ruby Isle 2205 North Calhoun Road, Brookfield
Monday-Friday 10:00-6:00, Saturday 10:00-5:00

262 780-0909

1

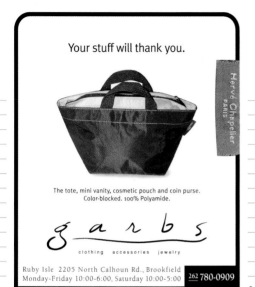
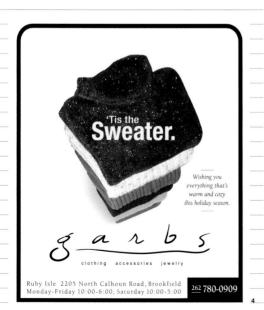
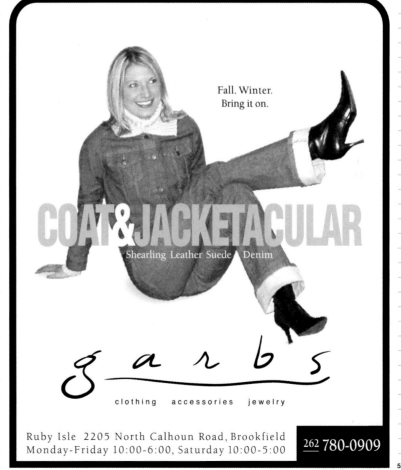

Richard Hollis in *Graphic Design: A Concise History* describes the poster as the essence of graphic design. Often described as an art form, the poster has long been a form of communication and is an integral part of our culture.

Exercise

Poster & Display

- Design a poster promoting a philosophy lecture that is part of a series organised by The Aristotelian Society.
- The poster will be displayed in schools, colleges, universities and libraries, and the client wants to use quotations from the philosophers featured in the series. It is therefore important that the quotation can be read relatively easily, but at the same time you should try to evoke the meaning of the quote in the way you design the poster.

From the early bill posters of the nineteenth century, which demonstrated the early struggles of the trade unions, to the later graphic use of letterforms throughout Europe and the USA, the development of posters offers us a contemporary view of history.

Well designed posters need to work on two levels: first, they need to attract attention; second, they need to inform. A good poster will meet these criteria and at the same time create a sense of form and illustrate good use of colour. The poster is a big canvas to work on and this gives you the chance to exploit the use of letterform as image.

One of the most important things to remember about posters is that the main message has to be immediate. Posters are often given no more than a quick glance in passing (think of roadside adverts, for example). For a book cover you can afford to have small type, because it will be read from a distance of about 15–20cm. Small type is definitely not acceptable in poster design. For the same reason, do not include too many different elements: make your point quickly and strongly through your use of form and colour. If you look at the most effective posters, you will see that a single, strong element is almost always more successful than a number of different elements. Audiences appreciate clarity and feel comfortable when they can assimilate an idea and information relatively easily.

In most cases, relatively few copies of posters are printed. (Silk) screen printing is a good option because it produces vivid colours, gloss and metallic inks. It can also print light colours on dark paper. If thousands of copies are being printed, then an offset litho process could be used; the colours tend to be flatter but the process is excellent at producing four-colour designs.

"Cogito ergo sum"

"Cogito ergo sum"

"Cogito ergo sum"

"Cogito ergo sum"

"Cogito ergo sum"

"Cogito ergo sum"

"Cogito ergo sum"

"Cogito ergo sum"

"Cogito
ergo sum"
(I think, therefore I am)

RENÉ DESCARTES *1596–1650*

"Cogito
ergo sum"
(I think, therefore I am)

RENÉ DESCARTES *1596–1650*

- The elements you have to work with are your choice of letterform, the way you arrange the copy in terms of line endings, composition, use of colour and the setting style.
- Select one of the following quotations:
  'No man's knowledge can go beyond his experience' John Locke 1632–1704.
  'Cogito ergo sum (I think, therefore I am)' René Descartes 1596–1650.
  'The world is everything, that is the case' Ludwig Wittgenstein 1889–1951.

'The heart of man is made to reconcile the most glaring contradictions' David Hume 1711–1776.
'Is that which is holy loved by the gods because it is holy, or is it holy because it is loved by the gods?' Plato 427–347 BC.
- Now add the rest of the copy:
  'The Aristotelian Society lecture series begins with [name of philosopher you have chosen] on [date]. For further details, contact the Secretary at the [name of university].'

- Pin your finished visual to a wall and step back a good distance: the visual attractiveness of the design becomes apparent at this first viewing. Ask yourself whether any of the copy is difficult to discern and make any necessary adjustments.
- The ideas below will help you get started.

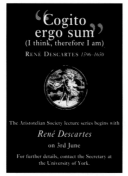

Poster & Display

Case Study

The message from this poster is clear. The graphic representation of drops of water immediately indicates the subject. The typeface that has been chosen is unfussy and does not conflict with the image.

1 A simple, yet effective, integration of text and image. Both are allowed to make their statement without interfering with each other.

2 The use of a bold sans serif typeface gives the copy strength. The type size is small so it does not compete with the image, but sits modestly in the background. The drops of water are centrally positioned, emphasising their central importance.

3–5 Here the designer has changed the background colours. This clearly shows the tremendous effect colour has on a design.

6 The poster that was eventually used has an extremely appealing colour scheme. There are no unnecessary words – the message is portrayed through the image. This design is attractive, simple and very memorable.

7 The knocked back, soft focus image gives this poster an abstract feel. The centrally positioned text is easy to read at a glance, despite its small size.

8 The eyes are the only element of this poster not covered in 'graffiti-style' writing. As such they draw the viewer's attention and the text becomes more imagistic than informational.

9–10 Both posters illustrate the winning formula of bright colours, simple image and minimal text.

Dia Nacional da Água

1 de Outubro 1998

SMAS
MUNICÍPIO DE ALMADA

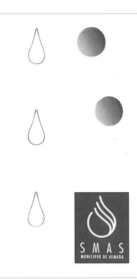
1

2

3

4

5

Professional Examples

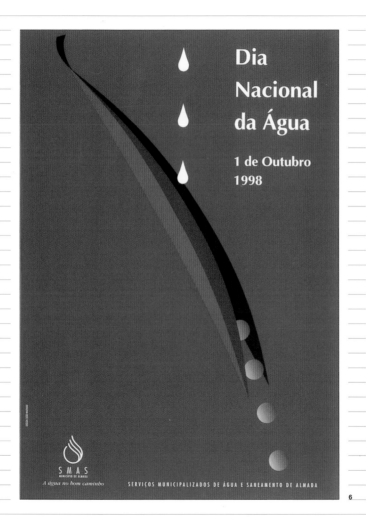

Dia
Nacional
da Água

1 de Outubro
1998

SMAS
MUNICÍPIO DE ALMADA
A água no bom caminho

SERVIÇOS MUNICIPALIZADOS DE ÁGUA E SANEAMENTO DE ALMADA

6

Design de Calçado 1996

7

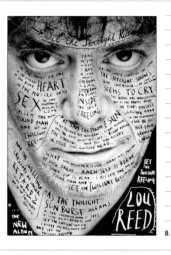

LOU REED

8

9

ÁGUA FONTE DE VIDA

10

Packaging & Labelling

Some packages are intended to be purely decorative while others, such as packs for medicinal material, need to convey important information. The design rationale is obviously very different for the two. In packs that contain information, clear typography is essential and you should concentrate on relaying the text as quickly and clearly as possible. Upper and lower case settings are easier to read than type set all in the upper case, just as range-left setting is easier than justified text. Avoid range-right settings, the use of italic or decorative fonts or reversed out type in any quantity. Try not to break words. For warnings and other important text, aim for maximum contrast in the colour schemes. You may well need to seek advice on the colour, particularly for people who suffer from colour blindness or impaired vision.

Decorative packaging gives you scope for imaginative uses of colour, type and illustration, and you can afford to experiment with the position of the copy. Asymmetric designs lend themselves to this category.

In some types of package design, you need to visualise how the design will work over the different planes. For example, you need to decide whether to have all copy and images flowing over from the front of the pack onto the sides. The contents of the packaging may determine which colour range you use. Very often the name of the product itself will give you some indication of what colour to select.

The way the packaging is produced is also something to think about as this can give a design an extra dimension. Cellophane, coloured tissues, cut-out shapes and ancillary printing techniques, such as lamination and varnishing or debossing and embossing, are all options to consider.

Having made your design decisions, try them out on a three-dimensional mock-up. This will show both you and the client how the whole design will look.

- Design the surface packaging and label for either 'Formula Perfume' or 'Ryder's Aromatherapy Candles'.
- The packaging should be modern and funky rather than sophisticated – designed for the new millennium consumer.
- Both items are mid-range in terms of price.
- The size and shape of the package is at your discretion – remember it must fit the product.
- Use four colour.
- Do several mock-ups before you decide upon a final version. Make sure the design you choose will be practical in terms of production and transportation.
- Make the pack up into a complete three-dimensional form.
- The ideas below will help you get started.

$$E = mc^2$$
$$a^2 = b^2 + c^2$$
$$x = 2y + z$$

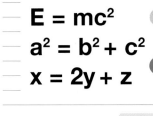

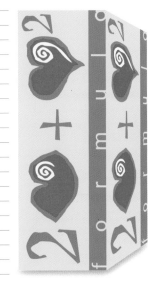

Packaging & Labelling

Case Study

This virtual gallery CD, which promotes photographers from diverse cultures through exhibitions, publishing and residency programmes, is a good example of layering information. The packaging reflects the multi-layering of the contents through the use of a clear acrylic CD case and translucent paper for all printed information.

1 Bold colours used for the CD and the package allow the name to stand out. A sans serif typeface is used so that reverse out of black is possible.

2 The overall package has a modern, exciting feel that reflects the content.

3 Clean, straight lines in colours that lie close on the colour wheel give the bags a sophisticated look.

4 The mixture of vertical and horizontal text setting works with the other elements of the packaging to create a well-balanced design – the vertical "juice" trademark complements the splash central image and the horizontal text harmonises with the placement of the tool itself.

5 A trendy matchbox that is a perfect example of packaging describing contents.

6 A busy, funky design – a veritable explosion of shapes and colour. This reflects the product – an explosion of sound.

7 This is well coordinated CD labelling and packaging. The tiny photographs on a white background give a harmonised feel that is supported by the peaceful atmosphere illustrated in the photographs.

1

2

Professional Examples

3

4

5

6

7

Home Page & Links

When you make any decision, think about the possibility that the site may expand in the future. This may be the time to implement a naming structure for your files; as a site grows, it can be difficult to keep track of everything if it is not well organised. For example, it is sensible to share the filename within a document and its associated assets – so if a document is called home.htm, then an embedded Flash file should be called home.swf.

Remember that your visitors will not navigate just one way through the site, but may go backwards and forwards between different points. They may also enter your site by following a link from another site, rather than via the home page. For this reason, you may want a simple navigation system that can appear on every page. It is an accepted convention that the corporate logo always takes you back to the home page when you click on it. This logo is generally shown on the upper left-hand corner, with the site navigation directly below or following across the top of the page.

Having navigation in this form means that it is always visible: you can always see the top left corner of a screen, but if someone has a screen that is smaller than the web page, then anything on the bottom right will disappear and they will have to scroll to find it.

A link connects one page with another. Links within a page are normally shown in a lighter colour than the main copy when unvisited and darker when visited. Conventionally, a link is underlined, although it need not be so. What is more important is that you do not emphasise standard text in a way that makes it look like a link, by underlining it or using colour, for example. Generally use weight to emphasise text.

Page size

As it is not possible to control the page size (there is unlimited vertical scroll as well as unlimited horizontal scroll), the layout should adjust to the monitor size. This is generally done by using borderless (and therefore invisible) tables.

Type

Remember that a web page is an animated medium and the visitor will leap through the pages rather than reading them in a linear fashion like a book. Any copy is generally shorter and more concise than it would be in a printed form, as people don't like to scroll up or down the page or strain their eyes. The font you choose should complement your overall design which is likely to include a core web font, such as those included with Microsoft Internet Explorer, for the copy.

Colour

Although print pages are generally printed using CMYK (see page 62), a computer screen shows colour as RGB (the additive reproduction process that mixes various amounts of red, green and blue to produce other colours). Depending on the user's monitor depth, anything from 256 to over a million colours can be shown. Without programming, you cannot determine the user's depth so it is best to limit yourself to 256 colours. Of these 256 colours, only 216 are available on both Mac and PC platforms. The 216 is referred to as the Web Safe Palette, and is available in all modern layout applications. This 216 palette should be exported as a GIF (graphics interchange format). For photographs, gradients and other continuous tone images, use the JPEG (joint photographics expert group) format to avoid banding.

Layout

You should avoid using columns, as the user would have to continually scroll up and down. You can, however, have sidebars, which often link to other relevant text, and this is an effective use of white space.

Conversion

After you have designed your layout it must be assembled as HTML, using a web graphics creation tool such as Macromedia Fireworks or Adobe Image Ready. These programs will convert your layout into tables that a browser can render. Try to avoid a big file size: a single page should not exceed 50k. Your website should embrace all current browsers and platforms. It is bad design to suggest that your user should download a specific browser in order to view your content.

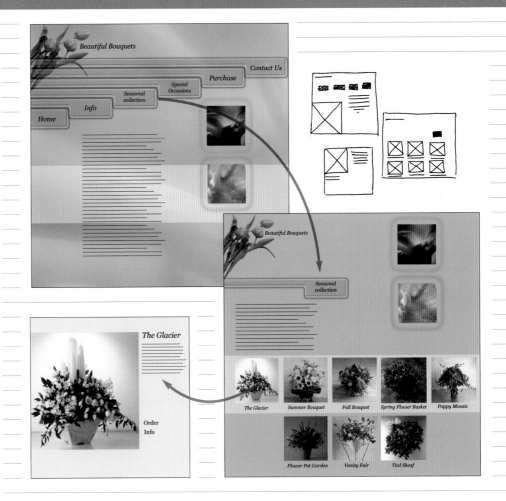

Internet sites are only successful if the viewer can navigate without difficulty from one point of the site to another. This is why it is important that certain elements such as navigation tools remain in similar positions and in the same style throughout the site.

Home Page & Links

Case Study

The client here – a photographic agency – wanted a clean and stylish site that would reflect the nature of their business. Text is kept to a minimum, and the emphasis throughout is on the pictures. The imagery is cropped and manipulated and the image frames are reproduced at different sizes. Animations within the page, both independent and mouse-driven, give the site a playful and creative feel.

1 **The client wanted a sexy opening screen that would generate excitement.**

2 **To give maximum impact, blurred still frames were inserted between other stills. This creates the illusion of speed not achievable with Flash alone.**

3 **The central position of the navigation is intended to give good balance to the layout, but users can drag and drop the menu to any location on the screen. A frosted panel appears against darker backgrounds to ensure that menu items always remain legible.**

4 **When moved, the menu swings like a pendulum, and continues to swing when it comes to rest.**

5 **This screen shows the potential for using images at full size. It also shows how subtle the navigation is. With the menu relocated to the left of the screen the user is not interacting with the navigation and the focus is wholly on the photographer's work. The two squares to the left of the photo are 'next' and 'back' buttons to change images within a section. The briefcase icon in the bottom left corner is the log-off button.**

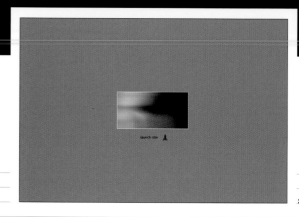

2

3

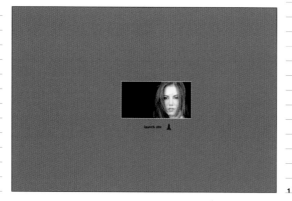

1

4

5

8

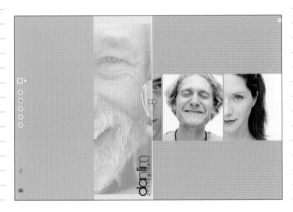

6

9

7

6 Clicking the 'next' or 'back' buttons causes the current image to be 'wiped' off the screen to reveal an image below.

7 This shows the transition between images when moving forwards or backwards within the same section. In this example, the translucent 'wiper' is on its way in.

8 Existing clients can enter a password-protected, personalised and database-driven area of the site to leave sticky notes as part of the sign-off process.

9 Clicking the Contact option on the menu brings up a screen where visitors can leave their contact details. It's much more user friendly to have forms in Flash than HTML because it is possible to submit the form and stay in the interface for confirmation.

Home Page & Links

Professional Examples

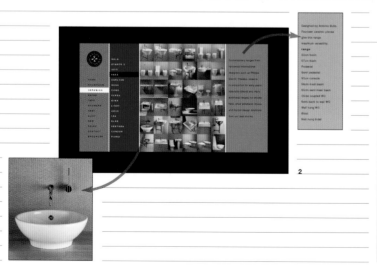

1 The home page for this specialist bathroom retailer is clearly laid out. The design has a modern feel, supported by the central image. The logo appears in the top left corner of every page, with the links always immediately underneath, making it very easy to access every page from any location.

2–3 Each page follows the same basic design and focuses on a simple message. This is a sophisticated and well thought-out site.

4–7 This site for the advancement of veterinary research requires the Flash plug-in. It's a funky, colourful, animated site. Circles form the basis of the design, from the vertical, curved link list on the left, to the circular text boxes, which scroll up and down as you hover over the red and white circles on the right. Despite the constantly moving circular images and complicated structure, it is easy to navigate around the site.

8–10 This site for a photo library of flowers, plants and trees goes for the simple approach. The background colours are muted and the site has a calm feel – perfect to represent nature photography.

4

8

5

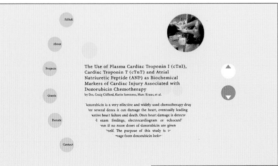

6

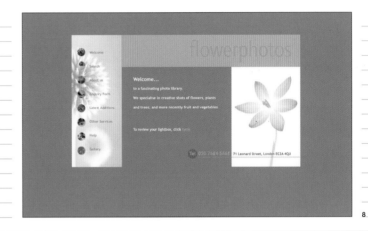

9

7

10

Presentation to Client

Of course, traditional skills still play an important part in presentation. Cutting mats for backgrounds, putting together spreads and generally manipulating the elements that make up a design are all part and parcel of a neat presentation. Psychologically, it is crucial that the presentation is of a high standard because it is at this point, the first viewing, that a good or bad impression is made.

One of the most important questions to ask at the briefing is what level of presentation the client expects. If he or she is visually aware, a 'rough' presentation in the form of black-and-white prints pasted together may be all that is required. For other clients, only full-colour print-outs will do. Whichever way you decide to proceed, discuss time and cost with the client. How many presentations would he or she like to see? You should budget for this in your overall estimate of cost. Establish how much of the job needs to be shown. Obviously if the brief is to design a range of stationery with a logo, this can be readily accommodated – but do you need to present every page of an 84-page brochure?

When you present your design, go back to the original briefing to establish that the decisions you have made fit in with the original proposals. As a designer you have to develop good communication skills, because this is how you sell your work. You must learn to listen and respond to comments in a positive way. Of course mistakes will happen— but it is the way you respond to mistakes and criticism that is important. If clients can see that you have endeavoured to solve the problem, it is far easier to resolve any issues amicably.

Finally, when you present your work make sure that every part of the project is clearly labelled and in the correct sequence. Time spent prior to the presentation is worth double or treble afterwards.

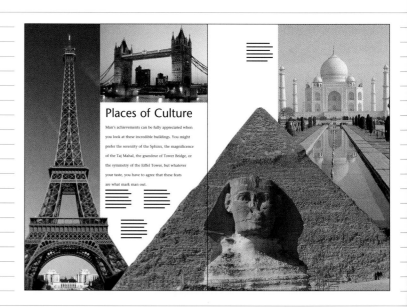

Places of Culture

Man's achievements can be fully appreciated when you look at these incredible buildings. You might prefer the serenity of the Sphinx, the magnificence of the Taj Mahal, the grandeur of Tower Bridge, or the symmetry of the Eiffel Tower, but whatever your taste, you have to agree that these feats are what mark man out.

- For this exercise take the project you have completed for the brochure or magazine exercise and present it to a colleague in three stages.
- First, go back to basics and sketch out the initial ideas on a piece of paper.
- Then put together a rough presentation. This is the basic layout structure without images or text.
- This should lead on to the fully finished presentation, with all the elements combined into one seamless project in full colour.
- Present your project to a friend or colleague. Explain the different stages you went through to get to the final version.
- The ideas below will help you get started.

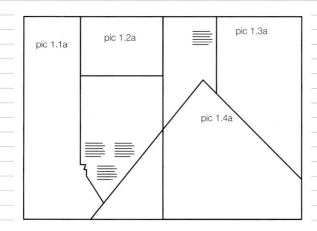

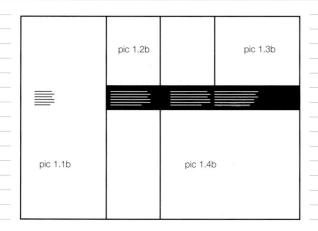

Index